D0180067

THE MYSTERY OF CHRIST

THE MYSTERY OF CHRIST

THE LITURGY AS SPIRITUAL EXPERIENCE

THOMAS KEATING

AMITY HOUSE
Amity, New York

Published by Amity House Inc.
106 Newport Bridge Road
Warwick, NY 10990

© 1987 by St. Benedict's Monastery

All rights reserved. No part of this publication may be reproduced or transmitted, in any form or by any means, without permission in writing from the publisher.

Library of Congress Catalog Card Number 87-72464

ISBN 0-916349-41-1

Contents

Preface

Christian spirituality and theology cannot be separated. God has joined them together in an indissoluble bond. The liturgy enshrines and manifests this vital unity. It is designed above all to transmit "the mind of Christ"[1], the consciousness that Jesus manifested of the Ultimate Reality as "Abba," the God of infinite compassion. "Abba" is, at one and the same time, totally transcendent and totally concerned about the human condition. When those who participate in the liturgy are disposed by adequate preparation and understanding, this experience of God, in ever-increasing degrees, is transmitted.

This transmission may take place by way of insight into the Mystery of Christ, of an infusion of divine love, or of both at once. It can also take place beyond any psychological perception in the darkness and immediacy of pure faith. In the latter case, it is known only by its fruits in our lives. In whatever way the transmission of the Mystery of Christ takes place, it is always recognized as sheer gift or grace. In the context of the Mystery of Christ and our participation in it, grace is the presence and action of Christ not only in the sacraments of the church and in prayer, but also in everyday life.

Contemplative prayer is the ideal preparation for liturgy. Liturgy, in turn, when properly executed, fosters contemplative prayer. Together they further the ongoing process of conversion to which the Gospel calls us. They

1

awaken us to the realization that we ourselves, as members of Christ's Body, are the cutting edge of the New Creation inaugurated by Christ's resurrection and ascension.

In the retreats of which these conferences were a part, four to five hours each day were devoted in common to contemplative prayer following the centering prayer method. Contemplative prayer in common is a powerful bonding experience as well as a profound form of liturgy. The daily practice of contemplative prayer, whether in common or in private, refines the capacity to listen to the word of God at ever deeper and more receptive levels of attentiveness. When the word of God in scripture and the sacramental rites have worked their way through our senses and reflective apparatus and penetrated to the intuitive level of our being, the immense energies of the Spirit are released, and our consciousness is gradually transformed into the mind of Christ.

The meaning of the terms in the title of this book may need explanation. The Greek word "mysterion," translated into Latin as "sacramentum," is translated in English as either "mystery" or "sacrament." In the context of the liturgy, these two words are synonymous and refer to a sacred sign or symbol — person, place, or thing — of a spiritual reality that transcends both the senses and the rational concepts that depend on them.

For example, the historical life and activity of Jesus are signs of the presence of the Eternal Word of God with whom his humanity was indissolubly united. That this union actually took place is the primary content of the Christian faith. How it took place is the Mystery of the Incarnation. When we speak of the "Mysteries" of Christ, we refer to his redeeming activities, especially his passion, death and resurrection, and the sacraments which prolong his activities in time through the ministry of the church. These visible, verifiable actions are signs that contain his presence and action here and now. Whenever and wherever the action of Jesus takes place, the life of God is transmitted.

THE POWER OF RITUAL

A large crowd followed, pushing against Jesus. There was a woman in the area who had been afflicted with a hemorrhage for twelve years. She had received treatment at the hands of doctors of every sort and exhausted her savings in the process. She got no relief; on the contrary, she only grew worse. She had heard about Jesus and came up behind him in the crowd and put her hand to his cloak. "If I just touch his clothing," she thought, "I shall get well." Immediately her flow of blood dried up and the feeling that she was cured of her affliction ran through her whole body.

Jesus was immediately conscious that healing power had gone out from him. Wheeling about in the crowd, he began to ask, "Who touched my clothing?"

His disciples said to him, "You can see how this crowd hems you in, yet you ask, who touched me?" Despite this, he kept looking around to see the woman who had done it.

Fearful and beginning to tremble now as she realized what had happened, the woman came and fell in front of him and told him the whole truth. He said to her, "Daughter, it is your faith that has cured you. Go in peace and be free of this illness." [Mark 5:28-35]

The woman afflicted with a hemorrhage was part of an immense crowd pushing against Jesus as he tried to make his way. This incident points to the meaning of ritual. Rituals are symbols, gestures, words, places and things that have a sacred meaning. They are the clothing of God, so to speak, and are saturated with the healing power of God. God, of course, does not wear clothes. Jesus, the Son of God made human, did wear clothes. And so, by touching the tassel of his cloak, this long-suffering woman was cured.

There is an intriguing analogy between her humble faith and what we do when we celebrate the liturgy. Notice that when the woman touched the clothing of Jesus, healing power went out from him. Healing power is going out from Christ when one approaches sacred rituals with faith; one is knocking at the door of his healing power and manifesting the measure of one's faith. Of course, ritual can become mere routine. Then it is an effort to renew one's faith in its healing power.

It is also possible to overdo ritual by the excessive multiplication of rites. Too many tassels or too few hinder the transmission of the healing power inherent in the discreet use of ritual. The sacred rites, like the garments of Jesus, do not have power of themselves. They merely clothe the reality concealed in them. To touch Jesus, we must not avoid the rituals or try to circumvent them, but go through them to the reality of his Presence. Ritual as a discipline is meant to sensitize our faculties to the sacredness of all reality.

There is an immense variety of ritual in the official worship of the church.

The Liturgical Year is the most comprehensive and profound of them all.

The Liturgical Year focuses on the three great theological ideas that form the heart of Christian revelation: divine light, life and love. They constitute the gradual unfolding of what we mean by grace, God's gratuitous sharing of his nature with us. As the primary focus of divine activity, each emphasizes a special stage or aspect of God's self-communication. These theological ideas are all contained in condensed form in each celebration of the Eucharist. In the Liturgical Year they are expanded in order to be studied and savored one by one, the better to search out and assimilate the divine riches contained in each of them. This marvelous arrangement enhances the power of the Eucharist to transmit them. Divine light is then experienced as wisdom, divine life as empowering and divine love as transforming.

TRANSMITTING THE MYSTERY OF CHRIST

When time began, the Word was there and the Word was face to face with God, and the Word was God. This Word when time began was face to face with God. All things came into being through Him and without Him there came to be not one thing that has come to be. In Him was life and the life was the light of humankind. The light shines in the darkness and the darkness did not lay hold of it.

There came upon the scene a man, a messenger from God whose name was John. This man came to give testimony on behalf of the light that all might believe through him. He was not himself the light; he was only to testify on behalf of the light.

Meanwhile, the true light which illumines everyone was making its entrance into the world. He was in the world and the world came to be through Him, and the world did not acknowledge Him. He came into his home and his own people did not welcome Him. But to as many as welcomed Him, he gave the power to become children of God. These are they who believe in his name, who are born not of blood or of carnal desire or of man's will. No, they are born of God. And the Word became a human being and lived among us, and we have looked upon His glory, such a glory as befits the Father's only-begotten Son, full of grace and truth. [John 1:1-14]

The prologue of John introduces us to the eternal plan of God in which Christ has the central position. The Eternal Word, the silence of the Father coming to full expression, has entered the world and manifested as a human being. Because of his infinite power, the Eternal Word has taken the entire human family into his divine relationship with the Father.

We who are incomplete, confused and riddled with the consequences of original sin constitute the human family that the Son of God took upon himself. The basic thrust of Jesus' message is to invite us into divine union, which is the sole remedy for the human predicament. Lacking the experience of divine union, we feel alienated from ourselves, God, other people and the cosmos. Hence, we seek substitutes for the happiness for which we are predestined but which we do not know how to find.

This misguided search for happiness is the human predicament that the Gospel addresses. The first word that Jesus speaks as he enters upon his ministry is "repent", which means, "change the direction in which you are looking for happiness." Happiness cannot be found in the programs fashioned in early childhood and based on instinctual needs for survival and security, affection and esteem, and power and control over as much of life as possible. These programs cannot possibly work in adult life, although everyone tries hard to make them workable. Happiness can be found only in the experience of union with God, the experience that also unites us to everyone else in the human family and to all reality.

This return to unity is the good news that the liturgy proclaims. It approaches us where we are. It engages our being with all its faculties and potentialities in a commitment to personal development and to the corporate development of the human family leading to the higher states of consciousness. The ripe fullness of this developmental process is what Paul calls the *pleroma*. The liturgy is the supreme vehicle for transmitting the divine life manifested in Jesus Christ, the divine-human being. When Jesus through his resurrection and ascension entered into his trans-historical life, the liturgy became the extension of his humanity in time. The feasts of the Liturgical Year are the clothes, so to speak, that make visible the Reality hidden but transmitted in sacramental rites.

The Liturgical Year was developed in the course of the first four centuries under the influence of the contemplative vision of the Gospel enjoyed by the Fathers of the church. It is a comprehensive program designed to enable the Christian people to assimilate the special graces attached to the principal events of Jesus' life. The divine plan according to Paul is to share with us the knowledge of the Father that belongs to the Word of God by nature and to the man Christ Jesus who was united to that Word. This consciousness is crystallized in Jesus' remarkable expression "Abba," translated "Father." "Abba" implies a relationship of awe, affection and intimacy. Jesus' personal experience of God as Abba is the heart of the Mystery that is being transmitted through the liturgy. The Liturgical Year provides the maximum communication of this consciousness. Each year it presents, relives and transmits the entire scope of the Mystery of Christ. As the process continues year after year, like a tree adding new rings to its growth, we grow toward maturity in Christ. And the expansion of our individual faith experience manifests the developing corporate personality of the New Creation called by Paul the "Body of Christ." The "Body of Christ," or simply "the Christ," is the symbol for Paul of the unfolding of the human family into Christ-consciousness, that is, into Christ's experience of the Ultimate Reality as *Abba.* Each of us, as living cells in the body of Christ, contributes to this cosmic plan through our own growth in faith and love and by supporting the same growth in others. Hence, the immense value of corporate worship and of sharing and celebrating the experience of the Mystery of Christ in a faith community.

The whole panorama of the mysteries of Jesus' life is condensed in a single Eucharistic celebration. The Liturgical Year divides up all that is contained in that single explosion of divine light, life and love so that we can more easily assimilate the significance of these theological ideas by experiencing them one by one. In the Christmas-Epiphany season, the focus is on the theological idea of light. In the Easter season, the focus is on the theological idea of life. In the Pentecost season, the focus is on the theological idea of love. Each of these theological ideas is communicated by means of a prolonged period of preparation leading up to the celebration of the principal feast. Each great theme is developed further in the feasts that follow, culminating in the celebration of the crowning feast of the season. We perceive the power of divine light, life and love when these great themes cease to be merely theological ideas and become our personal experience. This is the ultimate purpose of liturgy. Unlike other teachers, it transmits the knowledge that it expounds. Each year the Liturgical Year provides a complete course in moral, dogmatic, ascetical and mystical theology. More importantly, it empowers us to live the contemplative dimension of the Gospel — the stable and mature relationship with the Spirit of God that enables us to act habitually under the inspiration of the gifts of the Spirit both in prayer and action.

The Liturgical Year is an extraordinary production, addressing every level of our being at once and prodding our response. The liturgical texts for the various feasts and seasons are juxtaposed to bring out the spiritual significance of Jesus' life, death and resurrection. Insofar as the Liturgical Year is a course of Christian instruction, it might best be called "applied Scripture" because of its eminently practical character.

The Liturgical Year presents the events of Jesus' life in dramatic fashion. It commemorates them in a way similar to a documentary film. A documentary portrays real situations and thus engages us even more than drama.

Television offers an intriguing analogy to the way the liturgy commemorates the unfolding of Jesus' life as events that are happening here and now. For example, TV presents news or sports events live. Events that are happening on the other side of the world become present in one's living room. A liturgical celebration is not a live event in the ordinary sense since Jesus is no longer with us; rather, it makes the events of his life present spiritually through the communication of the grace attached to each of them and celebrated sacramentally. What happened twenty centuries ago is made present in our hearts. This television cannot do.

To continue this analogy, television coverage alternates close-up and long-distance shots. For example, in covering a sports event, the camera usually gives a panoramic view of the ball park and then a close-up, focusing on the action of a single player's performance. Then it returns to a long-distance shot and we see the crowd waving and cheering. This alternation of close-up and distance shots is precisely how the liturgy focuses our attention on the principal theological idea of each liturgical season. Each season presents us with an overview of the current theological idea, while the particular feasts within the season present close-ups of the action of Jesus in us and in the world.

For example, the Christmas-Epiphany Mystery begins with the season of Advent, an extended period of preparation that culminates in the climactic feast of Christmas. On the first Sunday of Advent, the liturgical camera gives us a broad view of the three-fold coming of Christ. On the following Sundays we are introduced to the three central figures of Advent: Mary, the Virgin Mother of the Savior; John the Baptist, who introduced Jesus to those who first heard his message; and Isaiah, who prophesied Christ's coming with extraordinary accuracy seven-hundred years before the event. The dispositions and behavior of these principals become living models for us to imitate. In this way, the liturgy awakens in us longings similar to those of the prophets who yearned for the coming of the Messiah. We are thus prepared for the spiritual birth of Jesus in us through our participation in the unfolding of the Christmas-Epiphany Mystery.

The series of feasts that follow the celebration of Christmas flesh out its profound significance. The grace of Christmas is of such magnitude that it cannot be grasped in one burst of light. Only with the celebration of the crowning feast of Epiphany is all that is contained in the theological idea of divine light fully revealed.

The entire scope of the mystery of Christ is experienced at ever-deepening levels of assimilation as we celebrate the liturgical seasons and their various feasts year by year. The liturgy does not offer us a mere seat in the bleachers, or even a ringside seat. We are invited to participate in the event itself, to absorb its meaning and to relate to Christ on every level of his being as well as our own. This developing relationship with Christ is the main thrust of the liturgical seasons and of their capacity to engage all our faculties: will, intellect, memory, imagination, senses and body. The transmission of this personal relationship with Christ — and through him with the Father — is what Paul calls the *Mysterion*, the Greek word for mystery or sacrament, an external sign that contains and communicates sacred Reality. The liturgy teaches and empowers us, as we celebrate the mysteries of Christ, to perceive them not only as historical events, but as manifestations of Christ here and now. Through this living contact with Christ, we become icons of Christ, that is, manifestations of the Gospel in the shifting shapes, forms and colors of daily life.

The consciousness of Christ is transmitted to us in the liturgy according to our preparation. The best preparation for receiving this transmission is the regular practice of contemplative prayer, which refines and enhances our capacity to listen and to respond to the word of God in scripture and in the liturgy. The desire to assimilate and to be assimilated into Christ's inner experience of the Ultimate Reality as Abba also characterizes contemplative prayer.

The liturgy is God's way par excellence of transmitting Christ-consciousness. It is the chief place where it happens. It makes use of ritual to prepare the minds and hearts of the worshipers. When we are properly prepared, it grasps our attention at every level of our being and the special grace of the feast is, in fact, communicated.

THE FIVE PRESENCES OF CHRIST IN THE LITURGY

The eleven disciples betook themselves to the mountain in Galilee to which Jesus had ordered them. When they saw him, they adored him, although at first they had doubts.

Jesus then came closer and spoke to them the following words, "Absolute authority in heaven and on earth has been conferred upon me. Go therefore and make all nations your disciples, baptizing them in the name of the Father and of the Son and of the Holy Spirit. Teach them to observe all the commandments I have given you. And mark: I am with you at all times, as long as the world will last." [Matt. 28:16-20]

This passage is the commission Jesus gave to the apostles to extend his teaching and experience of the Father throughout the world and throughout all time.

As has been noted, the liturgy expresses the whole of the Mystery of Christ in the celebration of a single Eucharist. In the Liturgical Year the treasures that are contained in a single Eucharist are separated from this profound unity and celebrated individually in the course of a yearly cycle. In the liturgy, eternal time penetrates each moment of chronological time. Eternal values breaking into chronological time are made available to us in the present moment. It is in this sense that Christ is present throughout all of time — past, present and to come. He is present to us insofar as we are present to the present moment. The present moment transcends all time and, at the same time, manifests eternity in chronological time. The *kairos* is the moment in which eternity and our temporal lives intercept. In the perspective of the *kairos*, time is time to grow and to be transformed, time also for the Christian community to spread throughout the world and to become the *pleroma*, the fullness of time when Christ will be all in all.[2]

The present moment as an encounter with Christ is celebrated in a special way in each Eucharist. Each Eucharist gathers together all the different ways in which Christ is present to us throughout our evolving chronological lives. The Eucharist is the celebration of the unfolding of our chronological lifetimes into the fullness of the Christ-life within us and of our transcendent potential to become divine.

Every time we celebrate the Eucharist five distinct presences of Christ are available.[3]

The first presence of Christ occurs when we gather together in his name to worship him and the Father whom he manifests. Just by gathering together to acknowledge or worship Christ, the Christian community makes Christ present. Any group gathered together in his name becomes itself a center of Christ's presence: "Where two or three are gathered together in my name, there I am among them." This truth is manifested in several of the appearances of Jesus after his resurrection. On one occasion while the disciples were gathered together for fear of the authorities, with the doors locked and barred, Jesus suddenly appeared in their midst. Where did he come from? Perhaps he came right out of the center of their hearts and materialized in bodily form. At first they thought he was a ghost and were afraid. Perhaps they were even more afraid that if he could get in, so could the authorities. In any case, when we gather together for prayer and enter the place of worship, Jesus enters with us in his glorified body, ready to flood each of us, according to our openness to his coming, with the riches of divine light, life and love.

The second way that Christ is present in the Eucharist is during the proclamation of the Gospel. Lectors are not only communicators of the sacred texts, but of Christ himself. This fact is strikingly exemplified in Christian history. Many persons have experienced a direct call from Christ to total commitment upon hearing a particular Gospel text proclaimed in the liturgy. The words of the Gospel have power to reach hearts. Each time the Gospel is proclaimed, the text has the potential to communicate what the Spirit is trying to say to us at this moment in our lives. When we connect with that message, we experience what Paul calls "a word of wisdom." A word of wisdom is not just a wise saying. It is a word that penetrates our hearts in such a way that we are inwardly aware that God is addressing us. Whether we like it or not, we know that the word of God, like a sword, has pierced our inmost being. It fills us with delight or profoundly challenges us, as the case may be. The power of the proclamation of the Gospel to communicate the presence and action of Christ requires that it be surrounded by rituals of special honor.

The third presence of Christ takes place during the Eucharistic prayer in which the passion, death and resurrection of Christ become present. The elements of bread and wine also represent the gift of ourselves. The consecration of these gifts into the body and blood of Christ signifies our incorporation as individual cells into the body of Christ, the New Creation of redeemed humanity that is gradually maturing over time into the fullness of Christ, the *pleroma*.

The fourth presence of Christ takes place in the communion service. At this moment the consecrated elements of bread and wine are presented to each of us to consume, in order that we, in turn, may be transformed into the larger organism of the body of Christ. The Spirit assimilates us into the body of Christ just as we assimilate the elements of bread and wine into our material bodies. The reception of the Eucharist is thus a commitment to open ourselves to the process of transformation into Christ. Christ in his human and divine nature comes to us in the Eucharist in Holy Communion not just for a few passing instants – for as long as the sacred species may remain undissolved in our digestive system – but forever. Moreover, each reception of the Eucharist sustains and increases the Presence that is already there from previous receptions. The presence of Christ that emerged from the community, that was proclaimed in the Gospel and that was made present in the Eucharistic prayer, now enters our bodies, minds and inmost being as we assimilate the Mystery of Faith.

Notice the ascending structure of these presences. Each one is more sublime than the previous one.

As marvelous as these gifts of Christ's presence are, they serve only to awaken us to the supreme Presence, the Presence that is already present. Although this Presence is not mentioned specifically in the *Constitution on the Sacred Liturgy*, it seems to be presupposed. All the sacraments, all prayer, all ritual are designed to awaken us to our Christ nature, out of which we and all our faculties are emerging at every microcosmic moment. Jesus, in commissioning the apostles, seems to speak to this experience: "Go and make all nations your disciples!" The Gospel of Mark expresses it more clearly: "Go into the whole world and preach the Gospel to all creation!"

Does this text refer only to the geographical world? This is the usual interpretation, but it does not exhaust the profound meaning of the text. We are invited, or more exactly commanded, to go into the expanding worlds that open to us as we move from one level of faith to the next. It is as if Jesus were to say, "Go forth from the narrow limits of your preconceived ideas and prepackaged value systems! Penetrate every possible level of human consciousness! Enter into the fullness of divine union and then, out of that experience, preach the Gospel to all creation and transform it through the empowerment which union and unity with me will instill in you."

Divine love makes us apostles in our inmost being. From *there* comes the irresistible presence and example that can transform the world.

I

The Christmas-Epiphany Mystery

Zachary, the father of John, filled with the Holy Spirit, uttered this prophecy:
"Blessed be the Lord the God of Israel, because he has visited and ransomed his people..." [Luke 1:67-68]
The "Visitation" of God is the experience of God's presence, the Ultimate Mystery making Itself known in the Word made flesh. This is the meaning of the Christmas-Epiphany celebration.

INTRODUCTION

The Christmas-Epiphany Mystery is the celebration of the transmission of divine light. The liturgical season begins with Advent, a period of intense preparation to understand and accept the three comings of Christ. The first is his historical coming in human weakness and the manifestation of his divinity to the world; the second is his spiritual coming in our inmost being through the liturgical celebration of the Christmas-Epiphany Mystery; the third is his final coming at the end of time in his glorified humanity.

On the feast of Christmas, the joyful expectancy exemplified by the Virgin Mary, John the Baptist and Isaiah — and shared by us in the Advent liturgy — come to fulfillment. Christ is born anew in our hearts through the increase of his light within us, and the consequences of our union with him begin to unfold.

In the feasts that follow, all that is contained in the explosion of divine light at Christmas is gradually revealed, culminating in the feast of Epiphany which is the fullness and crowning feast of the Christmas-Epiphany Mystery. In the clear light of Epiphany, faith in the divinity of Jesus and in our incorporation in him as members of his mystical body is the light (our guiding star) that empowers us to follow him and to be transformed into him.

While the theological idea of light still predominates on the feast of Epiphany, the theological ideas of divine life and love also appear, pointing to the great mysteries of Easter and Pentecost yet to come. We experience by anticipation the life-giving grace of Easter and the transforming graces of Pentecost. The liturgy commemorates, along with the coming of the Magi, two other events which symbolize the graces of Easter and Pentecost: the Baptism of Jesus in the Jordan and the changing of water into wine at the Marriage Feast of Cana.

Jesus sought baptism at the hands of John not for himself, but for us, the members of his mystical body. His descent into the waters of the Jordan prefigure his passion and death, and his rising out of the Jordan and the descent of the Spirit prefigure his resurrection and his gift of the Spirit at Pentecost. Thus, in the Baptism of Jesus the sacraments of Baptism and Confirmation are prefigured and bestowed in advance. He purifies his people and prepares them for union with himself.

The union established between Christ and us in Baptism and deepened by Confirmation is consummated in the Eucharist, the sacrament of divine union. The Eucharist and its transforming effects are prefigured by Jesus' changing water into wine at the Marriage Feast of Cana, while the wedding party symbolizes the joys of divine union, the ripe fruit of the transforming graces of Pentecost.

Here is a summary of the teaching of the liturgy in the Christmas-Epiphany Mystery:

> 1. Human nature is united to the Eternal Word, the Son of God, in the womb of the Virgin Mary: Advent.
> 2. The Eternal Word appears in human form as the light of the world: Christmas.
> 3. He manifests his divinity through his humanity: Epiphany.
> 4. By his baptism in the Jordan, he purifies the church, the

extension of his body in time, and sanctifies the waters of baptism: Epiphany and the Sunday following.

5. He takes his people to himself in spiritual marriage, transforming them into himself: Epiphany and the second Sunday following.

6. We study the practical consequences of being members of Christ's mystical body: the Second Reading for the Sundays in Ordinary Time following Epiphany.

THE CHRISTMAS-EPIPHANY MYSTERY

The word of God was spoken to John, son of Zachariah, in the desert. He went about the entire region of the Jordan proclaiming the baptism of repentance which led to the forgiveness of sins, as is written in the book of the words of Isaiah the Prophet: "A herald's voice in the desert, crying, 'make ready the way of the Lord, clear him a straight path.' " [Luke 3:2-4][1]

Advent is the celebration of the three comings of Christ: his coming in the flesh, which is the primary focus of the feast of Christmas; his coming at the end of time, which is one of the underlying themes of Advent; and his coming in grace, which is his spiritual coming in our hearts through the Eucharistic celebration of the Christmas-Epiphany mystery.

His coming in grace is his birth within us. This coming emphasizes the primary thrust of the liturgy, which is the transmission of grace, not just the historical commemoration of an event. Thus, the liturgy communicates the graces commemorated in the liturgical seasons and feasts. These center around the three great theological ideas contained in the revelation of Jesus: divine light, life and love. Each season of the liturgical year — Christmas-Epiphany, Easter-Ascension and Pentecost — emphasizes a particular aspect of the mystery of salvation, God's gratuitous self-communication. The rest of the Liturgical Year flows from these major themes and investigates their practical implications.

The Liturgical Year begins with the theological idea of divine light. And what is this light? You find out by attending the liturgy, provided you are properly prepared and provided that the liturgy is sensitively and reverently executed.

Each liturgical season has a period of preparation that readies us for the celebration of the climactic feast. The feast of Christmas is the first burst of light in the unfolding of the Christmas-Epiphany Mystery. Theologically, Christmas is the revelation of the Eternal Word made flesh. But it takes time to celebrate and penetrate all that this event actually contains and involves. The most we can do on Christmas night is gasp in wonderment and rejoice with the angels and the shepherds who first experienced it. The various aspects of the Mystery of divine light are examined one by one in the days following Christmas. The liturgy carefully unpacks the marvelous treasures that are contained in the initial burst of light. Actually, we do not grasp the full import of the Mystery until we move through the other two cycles. As the divine light grows brighter, it reveals what it contains, that is, divine life; and divine life reveals that the Ultimate Reality is love.

Epiphany is the crowning feast of Christmas. We tend to think of Christmas as the greater feast, but in actual fact, it is only the beginning. It whets our appetite for the treasures to be revealed in the feasts to come. The great enlightenment of the Christmas-Epiphany Mystery is when we perceive that the divine light manifests not only that the Son of God has become a human being, but that we are incorporated as living members into his body. This is the special grace of Epiphany. In view of his divine dignity and power, the Son of God gathers into himself the entire human family past, present and future. The moment that the Eternal Word is uttered outside the bosom of the Trinity and steps forth into the human condition, the Word gives himself to all creatures. In the act of creating, God, in a sense, dies. He ceases to be alone and becomes, by virtue of his creative activity, totally involved in the human adventure. He cannot be indifferent. Any theology that suggests that he is unconcerned is not the revelation of Jesus. On the contrary, the meaning of the life and message of Jesus is that the reign of God is "close at hand": the whole of God is now available for every human being who wants him.

Epiphany, then, is the manifestation of all that is contained in the light of Christmas; it is the invitation to become divine. Epiphany reveals the marriage between the divine and human natures of Jesus Christ. It also reveals God's call to the church (meaning us, of course) to be transformed by entering into spiritual marriage with Christ and to become fully human.

The coming of Christ into our conscious lives is the ripe fruit of the Christmas-Epiphany Mystery. It presupposes a presence of Christ that is already within us waiting to be awakened. This might be called the fourth coming of Christ, except that it is not a coming in the strict sense since it is already here. The Christmas-Epiphany Mystery invites us to take possession of what is already ours. As Thomas Merton put it, we are "to become what we already are." The Christmas-Epiphany Mystery, as the coming of Christ into our lives, makes us aware of the fact that he is already here as our true self — the deepest reality in us and in everyone else. Once God takes upon himself the human condition, everyone is potentially divine. Through the Incarnation of his Son, God floods the whole human family — past, present and to come — with his majesty, dignity and grace. Christ dwells in us in a mysterious but real way. The principal purpose of all liturgy, prayer and ritual is to bring us to the awareness of his interior Presence and union with us. The potentiality for this awareness is innate in us by virtue of being human, but we have not yet realized it. All three comings of Christ are built on the fact that we are in God and that God is in us; they invite us to evolve out of our human limitations into the life of Christ. Christ has come, but not fully: this is the human predicament. The completion of the reign of God (the *pleroma*) will take place through the gradual evolution of Christians into the mature age of Christ. Meanwhile, every human being and every human institution, however holy, is incomplete.

In the light of the Christmas-Epiphany Mystery, we perceive that union with Christ is not some kind of spiritual happy hour. It is a war with the powers of evil that killed Jesus and that might kill us, too, if we get in their way. Because we live in the human condition, the divine light is constantly being challenged by the repressive and regressive forces within us as individuals and within society, neither of which want to hear about love, certainly not about self-giving love. The Gospel message of service is not one that is easily heard. Hence, we need to deepen and nourish our faith through a liturgy that empowers us with the energy to go on showing love no matter what happens. This power is communicated to us in the Christmas-Epiphany Mystery according to our present receptive capacity.

THE ANNUNCIATION

> The angel Gabriel was sent from God to a town of Galilee named Nazareth, to a virgin betrothed to a man named Joseph, of the House of David. The virgin's name was Mary. Upon arriving, the angel said to her, "Rejoice, O highly favored daughter! The Lord is with you. Blessed are you among women."

She was deeply troubled by his words and wondered what his greeting meant. The angel went on to say to her, "Do not fear, Mary. You have found favor with God. You shall conceive and bear a son and give him the name Jesus. Great will be his dignity and he will be called Son of the Most High. The Lord God will give him the throne of David his father. He will rule over the House of Jacob forever and his reign will be without end."

Mary said to the angel, "How can this be since I do not know man?"

The angel answered her, "The Holy Spirit will come upon you and the power of the Most High will overshadow you; hence, the holy offspring to be born will be called Son of God. Know that Elizabeth your kinswoman has conceived a son in her old age; she who was thought to be sterile is now in her sixth month, for nothing is impossible with God."

Mary said, "I am the maid-servant of the Lord. Let it be done to me as you say." [Luke 1:26-38][2]

Advent is like the time of pregnancy when a new life begins to make itself known. The light of Christmas grows in each of us as the Advent season progresses, manifesting itself through flashes of insight that bring intimations of the dazzling light of the Christmas-Epiphany Mystery.

Mary is the key figure in Advent. In this text we hear the Angel Gabriel's announcement of her future motherhood. As far as we know, Mary was a girl of fourteen or fifteen, living in a backwater town. Nazareth did not have a good reputation judging by what Nathaniel had to say of it later: "Can anything goodcome out of that place?"[3]

It seems that Mary had been called by God to dedicate herself to him by a celibate commitment. At the same time, she was in the ambiguous position of being "engaged to a man named Joseph." We do not know the details of this relationship or what their agreement was. Celibacy was a rare choice in those days, especially for a woman. The fact that Mary was free to be innovative and flexible with respect to the popular expectations of her time and milieu is an indication of her spiritual maturity. Her choice of virginity presupposes a conviction about what God wanted her to do. She apparently persuaded Joseph to go along with this idea. In the Jewish customs of the time, she was already committed to be his wife by virtue of their engagement.

Then comes the surprise visit of the messenger of God. As many of the parables will later point out, God's action is unexpected. Sometimes the surprise is delightful, as when one finds a treasure hidden in a field. At other times, if God makes known some demand or challenge, the surprise is experienced as the end of one's world; one's little nest is shattered. Such events occur regularly in the lives of Mary and Joseph. This is only the first time that God, without being invited, intrudes into their lives and turns them upside down. The acceptance of what Jesus later preaches as the reign (or kingdom) of God involves the willingness to allow God to enter our lives in any way he pleases and at any moment — including now. Not tomorrow, but now! The reign of God is what happens; to be open to that reign is to be prepared to accept what happens. That does not mean that we understand what is happening. Most trials consist of not knowing what is happening. If we knew we were doing the will of God, trials would not bother us so much.

Here Mary is faced with one of God's favorite scenarios; it might be called the *double-bind*. The double-bind does not consist in the choice between what is obviously good and obviously evil — that is a temptation — but of not knowing which is good and which is evil. The dilemma may arise in another form: one cannot decide which of two apparent goods is God's will. For a delicate conscience, this causes deep trouble. The turmoil comes from wanting to do God's will and not knowing what it is. As a consequence, one feels torn in two directions at once. Two apparent but opposing goods demand one's total adherence, and both seem to be God's will. People on the spiritual journey regularly find themselves in such double-binds. They may even become more searching as the journey proceeds. This is the kind of dilemma that occurs in a vocational crisis such as, "Shall I enter a contemplative order? I have duties to others that seem to be important, and yet I feel a consistent call to solitude." The attraction to solitude in an active ministry is one of the classical double-binds in which those in active ministries often find themselves. Persons in cloistered communities experience the reverse.

Here is another scriptural example that shows how searching this trial may become.

John the Baptist had staked his integrity as a prophet on pointing to Jesus as the Messiah, the one who was to save his people from their sins. After John's confrontation with Herod, he was thrown into prison. He stands for everyone who suffers for the cause of justice and truth. In solitary confinement, separated from his disciples, he may have fallen into a depression. He began to have doubts about whether he had pointed out the right man. Jesus ate and drank with public sinners.Both he and his disciples did not observe the customary fasts. Could Jesus, who made friends with prostitutes and tax collectors and who encouraged the free and easy lifestyle of his disciples, really be the Messiah? Was John tempted to think, "Have I made a terrible mistake?" Here was a holy man nearing the end of his life, yet undergoing the worst crisis he had ever had to face.

Notice the agonizing double-bind. John had pointed to Jesus as the Messiah, but Jesus was not acting as the Messiah was expected to act. Accordingly, John sent his disciples to Jesus to ask, "Are you the Messiah or do we look for another?" The question suggests the full extent of the problem of conscience that he was enduring. Should he now disclaim the one he had previously proclaimed to be the Messiah? That was his great doubt. He could not decide which course to follow. So he sent his disciples to question the very person upon whose identity the he had staked his own prophetic mission — the one, to use his own words, "whose sandals he was not worthy to loose."

In the presence of John's disciples, Jesus worked a series of miracles that he knew would reassure John, fulfilling the prophesy of Isaiah which speaks of the blind receiving their sight and the poor having the Gospel preached to them. That was the resolution of John's double-bind.

Why did John suffer so terrible a trial right at the end of his life? The double-bind is sometimes designed to free us from the last vestiges of cultural conditioning, including our religious cultural conditioning. The means that we needed in the early part of our spiritual journey (but which we may have come to depend on too much) are gradually removed. One of the classical ways of removing them is a double-bind that forces one to grow beyond the limitations of one's culture, the influences of early childhood and one's early religious background. Family, ethnic and religious values are important and may support us for a certain time and to a certain place in the spiritual journey, but not to the place of total freedom that is God's ambition for each of us. Perhaps it was John's preconceived ideas about asceticism that God wanted to demolish in order to free him in the last days of his life to accept God's coming in any way at all, including through the eating and drinking and compassion of the actual Messiah.

Jesus, by the miracles he worked in the presence of John's disciples, thus said to John in answer to his question, "My friend, you did not make a mistake. I am the Messiah. But the Messiah is not limited to your ideas of what he should do and how he should behave."

That solved John's double-bind. Even holy people can be stuck in preconceived ideas or prepackaged value systems that are hard to let go. They may have strong expectations regarding how God should act or about how the spiritual journey and prayer should develop. War, persecution, bankruptcy, loss of a loved one, divorce, change of vocation, illness and death are all experiences that God uses to shatter their ideas or expectations.

When you are absolutely certain God wants two things that seem to be completely opposed, you are in a classical double-bind. Jesus himself endured the greatest double-bind there ever was in the Garden of Gethsemani. He, the innocent one, was asked to become sin for our sake; he who knew the goodness of God as no other human being has ever known or can know it, was asked to accept the inevitable result of identifying with our sins, namely, the sense of total alienation from God.

The experience of the double-bind hit Mary, as we saw, at the age of fourteen or fifteen. She had set up a plan for her life according to what she firmly believed was God's will. Along comes the Angel Gabriel and says, "God wants you to be the mother of the Messiah."

Mary was greatly troubled by the message of the angel. The underpinnings of her whole spiritual journey were shaken. She could not understand how God could have led her to believe that he wanted her to be a virgin and then be told by his messenger, "I want you to be a mother."

"How is this to be since I do not know man?" was Mary's response.

Notice the discretion of these words. She does not say she won't do it, but she delicately raises the problem of how it can be done since "I do not (and will not) know man." In other words, she takes her dilemma and respectfully places it in God's lap. "You created the problem," she seems to say, "Please solve it. I'm not saying yes. And, I'm not saying no. Please tell me how this problem is to be resolved."

The angel then goes on to explain, "The Holy Spirit will overshadow you." Her motherhood, in other words, is going to be outside the normal course of procreation. She will be able to consent to it because God is creating something absolutely unheard-of in human experience: a Virgin Mother.

The news the angel brought and its consequences completely disrupted Mary's plans for her life. Her mother soon became aware of her mysterious pregnancy. Joseph was so upset over it that he thought about giving her up. In other words, this pregnancy turned her life upside-down. Instead of being a respectable young woman engaged to Joseph, she now appeared to be someone who had engaged in premarital relations. She became one of the many disreputable people in her disreputable town. The same God who had inspired her to choose a celibate life made her the mother of the Messiah.

As human beings, we cannot presume that God will do something that has never been done before (although the angel said, "Nothing is impossible with God."). But we can be sure of that if we allow the creative energies of the double-bind to do their work, at some moment we will find ourselves in a higher state of consciousness. Suddenly we will perceive a new way of seeing all reality. Our old world view will end. A new relationship with God, ourselves and other people will emerge based on the new level of understanding, perception and union with God we have been given. The double-bind frees us to grow into an expanded relationship with all reality beginning with God. During Advent, as we celebrate the renewed coming of divine light, we receive encouragement to open to God's coming in any way that he may choose. This is the disposition that opens us completely to the light.

THE VISITATION

> Mary set out, proceeding in haste into the hill country to a town of Judah, where she entered Zechariah's house and greeted Elizabeth. When Elizabeth heard Mary's greeting, the baby stirred in her womb. Elizabeth was filled with the Holy Spirit and cried out in a loud voice: "Blessed are you among women and blessed is the fruit of your womb. But who am I that the mother of my Lord should come to me? The moment your greeting sounded in my ears, the baby stirred in my womb for joy. Blessed is she who trusted that the Lord's words to her would be fulfilled." [Luke 1:39-45][4]

We observed that Mary, after questioning the angel carefully, surmounted her double-bind by a leap of confidence. Her dilemma was resolved in an absolutely unexpected way by becoming simultaneously Virgin and Mother, demonstrating that there is no double-bind impossible for God to resolve. Even John the Baptist and Mary could not escape from God's enthusiasm to make them holier still. Difficulties give God the opportunity to refine and purify our motivation. They give us an opportunity to make a greater surrender.

God prepares us for the reception of his word the way a farmer tills a field in order to prepare it for the seed. God's preparation is like a tractor harrowing the field. Going one way, it tears up the soil and turns it over; going the other way it does the same as it criss-crosses the field. But everywhere it goes, it turns up new rocks buried unnoticed in the soil, each a possible destroyer of forthcoming seed.

Advent is a time of preparation. God prepared the soil of Mary's heart with incredible graces, culminating in the double-bind that enabled her to attain a new level of self-surrender. In order to bring forth in her body the Word of God, she first had to conceive and bring him forth spiritually. If you see somebody performing virtuous activity, this presupposes an enormous amount of preparation. He brought Mary to the point where he could fulfill his eternal plan. Paul says, "At the appointed time, God sent his Son, born of a woman."

Mary's union with God was so great that she was able to bring God physically into the world. All the images of the Old Testament referring to God's presence are crystallized in her. Having received the Word of God physically into her body, Mary contributed out of her human substance to the formation of the new divine-human person. The birth of Jesus was also the advent of a new aspect of time. The Greek word for "the appointed time" is *kairos*. The *kairos* is eternal time breaking into chronological time; it is vertical time cutting across horizontal time. As a result, the whole of the Mystery of Christ is totally available at every moment.

The liturgy celebrates certain special events in order to sensitize us to the fact that every moment is sacred. Time is time to grow, nothing else. Time is time to transform all the elements of life so that we can manifest Christ in our chronological lifetimes. The example of Mary is saturated with symbols of the most arresting kind to awaken us to the proper human response to the Eternal Word coming into chronological time and transforming it. The *pleroma* or "fullness of time" that Paul speaks of, when Christ will be "all in all," depends on our personal contribution as living cells in the body of Christ. The present moment is the moment in which eternity (vertical time) breaks into our lives. Thus, ordinary life, just as it is, contains the invitation to become divine.

Mary shows us, by the coming of the Eternal Word into her body, what to do with vertical time. Once we grasp the fact that the Word of God is living within us, we realize that we are not alone. We are lived in by God. God is living in us not as a statue or picture, but as energy ready to direct all our actions moment by moment. Hence, the necessity of a discipline of prayer and action to sensitize ourselves to the divine energy which Paul calls Spirit of the *pneuma* and which we translate as God.

What is Mary's first response to the gift of divine motherhood? She goes to see her cousin Elizabeth who happens to be having a baby and who needs help with whatever you do when you are getting ready for a baby: making diapers, preparing the bassinet, knitting little socks and bonnets. That is what she figured God wanted her to do. It never occurred to her to tell anyone about her incredible privilege. She simply did what she ordinarily did: she went to serve somebody in need. That is what the divine action is always suggesting: help someone at hand in some small but practical way. As you learn to love more, you can help more.

Mary did not go to counsel Elizabeth; she did not go to evangelize Elizabeth; she went to prepare the diapers. That is true religion: to manifest God in an appropriate way in the present moment. The angel had said that Elizabeth was soon to have a baby. Mary said, "Is that so? She must need help; I'll go at once." She went "in haste," manifesting her eagerness to be of service without any thought about her own condition, including, I presume, what Joseph or her mother were thinking about her unexpected pregnancy.

Mary entered the house of Elizabeth and said hello. The Presence that she carried within her was transmitted to Elizabeth by the sound of her voice. In response, the baby in Elizabeth's womb leapt for joy; he was sanctified by Mary's simple greeting. God's greatest works take place without our doing anything spectacular. They are almost side-effects of doing the ordinary things we are supposed to be doing. If you are transformed, everybody in your life will be changed too. There is a sense in which we create the world in which we live. If you are pouring out love everywhere you go, that love will start coming back; it cannot be otherwise. The more you give, the more you will receive.

Following Mary's example, the fundamental practice for healing the wounds of the false-self system is to fulfill the duties of our job in life. This includes helping people who are counting on us. If prayer gets in the way, there is some misunderstanding. Some devout persons think that if their activities at home or their job get in the way of praying, there is something wrong with their activities. On the contrary, there is something wrong with their prayer.

Contemplative prayer enables us to see the treasures of sanctification and the opportunities for spiritual growth that are present day by day in ordinary life. If one is truly transformed, one can walk down the street, drink a cup of tea or shake hands with somebody and be pouring divine life into the world. In Christianity motivation is everything. When the love of Christ is the principal motivation, ordinary actions transmit divine love. This is the fundamental Christian witness; this is evangelization in its primary form.

The early Christians seem to have taken evangelization in too literal a sense, preaching the word of God as if it were an end in itself. Because they were holy, their preaching had great effect, but not as great an effect as the witness of the martyrs of blood, and later, the martyrs of conscience. The essential thing, if one wishes to spread the Gospel, is the transformation of one's own consciousness. If that happens, and in the degree that it happens, one's ordinary actions become effective in communicating the Mystery of Christ to whomever comes into one's life.

A sanctified person is like a radio or TV station sending out signals. Whoever has the proper receptive apparatus can receive the transmission. What Mary teaches us by her visit to Elizabeth is that the sound of her voice awakened the transcendent potential in another person without her saying anything. She was simply Mary, the ark of the Covenant; that is, one in whom God was dwelling. Thus, when Mary said hello to Elizabeth, the child in her womb leapt for joy. His divine potentiality was fully awakened. So was Elizabeth's. She was filled with the Holy Spirit. This is the most sublime kind of communication. Transmission is not preaching as such. Transmission is the capacity to awaken in other people their own potentiality to become divine.

CHRISTMAS

In the beginning was the Word; the Word was in God's presence, and the Word was God. He was present to God in the beginning. Through him all things came into being, and apart from him nothing came to be. Whatever came to be in him, found life, life for the light of human beings. The light shines on in darkness, the darkness did not overcome it.

The real light which gives life to every person was coming into the world.

He was in the world, and through him the world was made,
yet the world did not know who he was. To his own he came,
yet his own did not accept him. Any who did accept him he
empowered to become children of God.

These are they who believe in his name — who were
begotten not by blood, nor by carnal desire, nor by anyone's
willing it, but by God.

The Word became flesh and made his dwelling among us,
and we have seen his glory, the glory of an only Son coming
from the Father, filled with enduring love. [John 1:1-14]

The feast of Christmas is the celebration of divine light breaking into
human consciousness. This light is so bright that it is impossible at first sight
to grasp its full meaning. Only an intuitive realization such as that of the
shepherds is able to enjoy it. Later, as our eyes adjust to the light, we perceive
little by little all that is contained in this Mystery, culminating in the crowning
feast of Epiphany, the manifestation of the divine in the Babe of Bethlehem.

Let us try to grasp the significance of the Word made flesh. The Greek
New Testament word for flesh is *sarx*. *Sarx* means the human condition
— the incomplete, unevolved, immature levels of human consciousness. It
means human nature in its subjection to sinfulness. Jesus did not merely
assume a human body and soul; he assumed the actual human condition
in its entirety, including the instinctual needs of human nature and the cultural
conditioning of his time.

Sarx refers to the human condition closed in on itself; fallen, and not
interested in rising. It is the human condition committed to biological survival
for its own sake or for the sake of the clan, tribe, nation or race.

The Greek word *soma* refers to the body insofar as it is open to further
evolution: it is the human condition open to development. "The Word was
made flesh" signifies that by taking the human condition upon himself with
all its consequences, Jesus introduced into the entire human family the
principle of transcendence, giving the evolutionary process a decisive thrust
toward God-consciousness.

In the *Epistle to the Romans*, Adam is the symbol of solidarity in the
flesh (*sarx*). Everybody shares the *sarx* of Adam and thus forms one corporate
personality with him. Christ, assuming the human condition exactly as it
is, penetrates it to its roots and becomes the source of a new corporate
personality open to transcendence. The Spirit, the principle of transcendence,

frees the human condition (*sarx*) for movement into the new corporate personality that Paul calls the Body of Christ. Our participation in the Body of Christ has a corporate and cosmic significance. To say "no" to that participation is the primary meaning of sin in the New Testament. It is the choice to remain just flesh (*sarx*), that is, to be dominated by the self-centered programs for happiness. It is to opt out of the divine plan for the transformation of human consciousness into Christ-consciousness. This transformation is what Christmas is all about. This is the growth process that the Gospel inaugurates and to which we are called. Self-centered human nature seeks out ever more and better ways to remain just as it is, because that seems to guarantee its survival. But to choose the status quo is to opt for solidarity with Adam and to reject "the Christ."

"To everyone who received him, he gave power to become the children of God," that is, to know their divine Source. This is the Mystery of the Word made flesh. *Flesh* does not merely mean skin and bones; it means the worldly *values* of the self-centered programs for happiness held firmly in place by conscious or unconscious habits or by overidentification with one's family, tribe or nation. Christ, by joining the human family, has subjected himself to the consequences of the flesh and at the same time introduced into it the principle of redemption from all pre-rational levels of consciousness. Our own development into higher states of consciousness is the cutting edge of the corporate personality of "the Christ," the gradual unfolding in time of the new Adam. Every act that is motivated by that vision — every healing of body, soul or social ill — is contributing to the growth of the Body of Christ and hence to the *pleroma*. This will occur when enough individuals have entered into Christ-consciousness and made it their own.

The joy of Christmas is the intuition that all limitations to growth into higher states of consciousness have been overcome. The divine light cuts across all darkness, prejudice, preconceived ideas, prepackaged values, false expectations, phonyness and hypocrisy. It presents us with the truth. To act out of the truth is to make Christ grow not only in ourselves, but in others. Thus, the humdrum duties and events of daily life become sacramental, shot through with eternal implications. This is what we celebrate in the liturgy. The *kairos*, "the appointed time," is *now*. According to Paul, "Now is the time of salvation," that is, now is the time when the whole of the divine mercy is available. Now is the time to risk further growth. To go on growing is to be at the cutting edge of human evolution and of the spiritual journey. The divine action may turn our lives upside-down; it may call us into various forms of service. Readiness for any eventuality is the attitude of one who has entered into the freedom of the Gospel. Commitment to the new world that Christ is creating — the new corporate personality of redeemed humanity — requires flexibility and detachment: the readiness to go anywhere or nowhere, to live or to die, to rest or to work, to be sick or to be well, to take up one service and to put down another. Everything is important when one is opening to Christ-consciousness. This awareness transforms our worldly concepts of security into the security of accepting, for love of God, an unknown future. The greatest safety is to take that risk. Everything else is dangerous.

The light of Christmas is an explosion of insight changing our whole idea of God. Our childish ways of thinking of God are left behind. As we turn our enchanted gaze toward the Babe in the crib, our inmost being opens to the new consciousness that the Babe has brought into the world.

EPIPHANY

The first text recalls the manifestation of Jesus in his divine Person to the Gentiles.

> After their audience with the king, they set out. The star which they had observed at its rising went ahead of them until it came to a stand still over the place where the child was. They were overjoyed at seeing the star, and on entering the house, found the child with Mary, his Mother. They prostrated themselves and did him homage. Then they opened their coffers and presented him with gifts of gold, frankincense, and myrrh. [Matt. 2:9-12]

The second text recalls the manifestation of Jesus in his divine Person to the Jews at the river Jordan.

> During that time Jesus came from Nazareth in Galilee and was baptized in the Jordan by John. Immediately, coming out of the water, he saw the sky rent in two and the Spirit descending on him like a dove. Then a voice came from the heavens: "You are my beloved Son. On you my favor rests." [Mark 1:9-11]

The third text recalls the manifestation of Jesus in his divine Person to his disciples at the wedding feast of Cana.

> There was a wedding at Cana in Galilee, and the mother of Jesus was there. Jesus and his disciples had likewise been invited to the celebration. At a certain point the wine ran out and Jesus' mother told him, "They have no more wine."
>
> Jesus replied, "Woman, how does this concern of yours involve me? My hour has not yet come."
>
> His mother said to the waiters, "Do whatever he tells you."
>
> As prescribed for Jewish ceremonial washings, there were at hand six stone water jars, each one holding twenty to thirty gallons.
>
> "Fill the jars with water," Jesus ordered, at which they filled them to the brim. "Now," he said, "draw some out and take it to the waiter in charge." They did as he instructed them. The waiter in charge tasted the water made wine, without knowing where it had come from; only the waiters knew, since they had drawn the water. The waiter in charge called the groom over and remarked to him: "Most people usually serve the choice wine first; then when the guests have been drinking awhile, a lesser vintage. What you have done is to keep the choice wine until now." Jesus performed this first of his signs at Cana in Galilee. Thus did he reveal his glory, and the disciples believed in him. [John 2:1-12]

These three readings are an integral part of the celebration of Epiphany, the crowning feast of the Christmas-Epiphany Mystery and the full revelation of all that the light of Christmas contains. The manifestation of Jesus in his divinity to the Gentiles in the persons of the Magi is supplemented by two other events that are manifestations of Jesus' divine nature from a later period in his life. The liturgy is primarily a parable of what grace is doing now; it disregards historical considerations and juxtaposes texts in order to bring out the sublime significance of what is being transmitted in an invisible way through the visible signs.

The first text describes the manifestation of Jesus' divinity to the Magi. They came from the ends of the earth and thus are symbols for all time of genuine seekers of the truth.

Jesus' Baptism in the Jordan and the Marriage Feast of Cana are integrated into the celebration in order to enlarge the perspective from which we perceive the divinity of Jesus. Jesus' baptism by John represents the manifestation of Jesus' divinity to the Jews, the moment when Jesus entered fully into his mission for the salvation of the human family. His baptism in the Jordan is a preview of the graces of Easter and Pentecost, in which we celebrate the Mysteries of divine life and love. Jesus' descent into the waters of the Jordan anticipates his descent into the sufferings of his passion and death; his emergence from the Jordan symbolizes his resurrection; and the Dove's descent prefigures the outpouring of the Holy Spirit at Pentecost.

All water has been sanctified by its contact with the body of Jesus in the Jordan. Moreover, every drop of water in the universe, in virtue of the baptism of Jesus, has become a vehicle of grace. Every kind of affliction, symbolized by the waters of the Jordan, has become a vehicle of grace. Even suffering that is the direct consequence of sin has become an inexhaustible source of grace. This does not mean that suffering is an end in itself, but that it has to be accepted, passed through and transcended. It is the touch — the presence — of Jesus which transforms suffering into a vehicle of sanctification.

The third text describes the Marriage Feast at Cana where Jesus manifested his divinity to his disciples.

Epiphany celebrates the marriage, so to speak, between the church and Christ; we, of course, are the church. Hence, the wedding feast is a symbol of the celebration of the divine nuptials in the souls of those who have experienced the divine light, and the divine life and love which that light contains. The new wine is the transcendent principle that Christ has brought into the world by taking human nature into himself. The whole human family is taken up into this new life, which has been inserted once and for all into the heart of God by the Incarnation and the redemptive work of Jesus. The new wine is the message of the Gospel, a message that announces that this process is happening. This is the greatest news there ever was! The human family has become divine! Through baptism we accept our personal invitation and, by struggling with the false-self system, gradually enter into the marriage chamber — the permanent awareness, through faith, of our union with Christ who takes us into the bosom of the Trinity. Since human beings were formed from the earth, the earth itself, represented by us and in us, is taken up into the Eternal Word. In human beings, God reaches the highest conceivable level of self-communication and gathers all that he has created into oneness with himself.

The final consummation, when "God will be all in all," takes place when the new wine has been served to everyone. The head waiter said to the young man, "You have saved the good wine until now." This is the wine of the Spirit that rejoices the hearts of all who drink it.

THE SIGNIFICANCE OF THE WEDDING FEAST AT CANA

There was a wedding at Cana in Galilee. The mother of Jesus was present. Jesus and his disciples had also been invited. When they ran out of wine, since the wine provided for the wedding was all finished, the Mother of Jesus said to him, "They have no wine." Jesus said, "Woman, why turn to me? My hour has not come yet." His Mother said to the servants, "do whatever he tells you."

There were six stone water jars standing there, meant for the purifications that are customary among the Jews. Each one held twenty or thirty gallons. Jesus said to the servants, "Fill the jars with water," and they filled them to the brim. "Draw some out now," he told them, "and take it to the chief steward." They did so. The chief steward tasted the water and it had turned into wine. Having no idea where it had come from (only the servants who had drawn the water knew), the chief steward called the bridegroom and said, "Most people serve the best wine first and keep the cheaper wine until the guests have had plenty to drink, but you have kept the best wine until now!"

This was the first of the signs given by Jesus. It was given at Cana in Galilee. He let his glory be seen and his disciples believed in him. [John 2:1-12][4]

Epiphany, as the celebration of the marriage of the Son of God with human nature, reveals the deepest significance of the Eternal Word becoming a human being. Furthermore, it is our personal call not only to the surrender of faith, but to transformation into divine life and love. The marriage feast, taking place in a tiny out-of-the-way town, becomes the symbol of the most fantastic event in human history, the most striking example of how eternal time enters into chronological time and transforms it. What happens when the wine begins to run out and the bridal couple are in danger of embarrassment, becomes a cosmic event. What Jesus does at the marriage feast is the symbol of what he will later accomplish through his passion, death and resurrection. The water stored in the jars is the symbol of the old Adam, of solidarity in human incompletion and sin. Jesus takes this water and transforms it into wine — not just into new water, but into something totally new! The sparkling, heady character of wine is the symbol of the experience of refreshment, enthusiasm and exhilaration that characterize the fruits of the Spirit.

The jars of water were required for purification according to Jewish custom, before, during and after the meal. Notice that each jar contained twenty to thirty gallons when filled to the brim. That is about a thousand quarts. After the miracle, there was wine enough to satisfy an army! The implication is that there is no limit to the new wine of the Gospel.

Who are the guests? You and I, of course. We see in this miracle the revelation of Christ's union with the human family, a marriage that is consummated in the Eucharist and that transports the guests into the New Creation. The corporate personality of the new humanity is called the Body of Christ. The Body of Christ grows through the process of our personal awakening to the divine life. Thus, everyone is invited to this wedding banquet. If we consent to participate, we receive the gift of the Spirit without measure, like the enormous superfluity of wine that Jesus provided for the embarrassed couple.

The three historical events singled out by the liturgy of Epiphany express this movement of incorporation into Christ and of transformation of consciousness.

1) The manifestation of the Babe's divine nature to the Magi signifies the call to divine union extended to every person — past, present and to come — in virtue of Christ's becoming a member of our race.

2) The manifestation of Jesus' divine nature to he Jews bythe voice from heaven after his baptism in the Jordan signifies our proximate call to divine union. The human family and each of us is purified by the waters of baptism and prepared for spiritual marriage with the Son of God.

3) Finally, the manifestation of Jesus' divine nature to the apostles through the transformation of water into wine at the marriage feast of Cana signifies the consummation of the spiritual marriage of Christ with human nature and with each of us in particular.

Each of these three ascending invitations depends, of course, on our consent. As living cells in the Body of Christ, we are caught up in the process that is moving toward the *pleroma.* This term describes the ripening development of Christ-consciousness shared by each of the individual cells in the corporate Body of Christ. This transcendent movement is like leaven in the dough, raising us out of our separate-self sense into the life of the Spirit, symbolized by the new wine.

We can cling to the old Adam and solidarity with him, or we can accept the Spirit inviting us to unlimited personal and corporate growth in Christ, the new Adam. This incredible invitation is signified by a joke.

Mary, the Mother of Jesus, takes note of the impending embarrassment of the couple and says to him, "They have no wine." Jesus replies, "My hour (*kairos*) has not yet come." As if to say, "My self-awareness as the Son of God has not yet come to term, and this act would anticipate it."

She says to the waiters, "Do whatever he tells you." Jesus acquiesces and tells the waiters to fill the jars with water and then to take some of it to the chief steward to taste. When the steward tasted the water now become wine, he was astonished. It was by far the best wine yet. He was so impressed that he went to the bridal couple and said, "Everybody serves the good wine first and then, when the guests are well satisfied, serves the wine they would like to get rid of. But you have saved the best wine until now!"

The joke is more than funny. It should keep us in joyful laughter for the rest of our lives and indeed, for all eternity. We should be doing cartwheels, jumping up and down, standing on our heads! Not even a liturgical dance meets the requirements of this feast. Divine Love is ours in superabundance. This is the light that is revealed as the gifts of the Magi, symbolizing the inner treasures of the Christ, are opened up. All these gifts are ours, right now, in the Eucharistic liturgy. The new wine of the Spirit is being served.

II

The Easter-Ascension Mystery

On that day you will know that I am in my Father, and you in me, and I in you. The one who obeys the commandments one has from me is the one who loves me; and the one who loves me will be loved by my Father. I too will love that person and reveal myself to that person [John 14:20-21].

INTRODUCTION

The theological ideas of divine life and love, anticipated in Epiphany, the crowning feast of the Christmas-Epiphany Mystery, now come into clear focus. Once again, there is a prolonged period of preparation (Lent) for the principal feast which is Easter. The Sundays after Easter develop the significance and fruits of Christ's resurrection, culminating in the crowning feast of the season, which is the Ascension.

LENT AND THE HUMAN CONDITION

The Spirit sent Jesus out toward the desert. He stayed in the wasteland forty days, put to the test there by Satan. He was with the wild beasts, and angels waited on him.

> After John's arrest, Jesus appeared in Galilee proclaiming
> God's good news: "This is the time of fulfillment. The reign of
> God is at hand! Reform your lives and believe in the good news!"
> [Mark 1:12-15][1]

Easter, with its grace of interior resurrection, is the radical healing of
the human condition. Lent, which prepares us for this grace, is about what
needs to be healed.

According to the evidence of developmental psychology, each human
being recapitulates the pre-rational stages of development toward full reflective
self-consciousness that the human family as a whole has undergone in its
evolutionary ascent. In the first six months of life, the infant is immersed
in nature and has no awareness of a separate identity. As the infant begins
to differentiate a body-self, its emotional life clusters around its instinctual
drives for survival/security, affection/esteem, and power/control. Image
patterns, emotional reactions and behavior gravitate around these instinctual
needs and create elaborate and well-defended programs for happiness (or
programs to avoid unhappiness) that might be called "energy centers". With
the gift of language, the child begins to internalize the values of parents,
peers and the prevailing culture, drawing its self-image, self-worth and value
system from the values and expectations of the group. This process of
socialization compounds the complex networking of the energy centers.

The greater the extent to which the infant or child feels deprived of
instinctual needs, the more its energies are invested in emotional programs
designed to satisfy one or all of these needs. When these programs for
happiness are frustrated, upsetting emotions such as grief, apathy, greed,
lust, pride or anger instantly arise. If these emotions are painful enough,
one is prepared to trample on the rights and needs of others, as well as
on our own true good, in order to escape the pain. This leads to the behavior
that we call personal sin. Personal sin is the symptom of a disease. The
disease is the false-self system: the gradual building up of the emotional
programs for happiness initiated in early childhood and expanded into energy
centers around which one's thoughts, feelings, reactions, mindsets, motivation
and behavior gravitate. As each new stage of developing human consciousness
unfolds, an increasing sense of separation emerges, along with the
corresponding feelings of fear and guilt. We come to full reflective self-
consciousness with the pervasive sense of alienation from ourselves, other
people, and God. We feel more or less alone in a potentially hostile universe.

We may even look back with longing to more primitive levels of awareness when we were able to enjoy life without self-reflection and hence without guilt feelings.

As we approach the age of reason, our developing self-consciousness finds itself at a crossroad: on one hand, the urge toward personhood and consequent responsibility; on the other, fear of increasing responsibility and the guilt feelings associated with it. But instead of evaluating our emotional programs for happiness, our rational faculties justify, rationalize and even glorify them. Into the human predicament — and the liturgical season of Lent — Jesus comes proclaiming, "Repent, for the reign of God is at hand".

"Repent" means "change the direction in which you are looking for happiness." The call to repentance is the invitation to take stock of our emotional programs for happiness based on instinctual needs and to change them. This is the fundamental program of Lent. Year by year, as the spiritual journey evolves, the destructive influences of these unevaluated programs for happiness become more obvious and, in proportionate manner, the urgency to change them increases. Thus the process of conversion is initiated and carried on. The term of this process is the experience of inner resurrection celebrated in the Easter-Ascension Mystery.

The Lenten liturgy begins with the temptations of Jesus in the desert, deal with the three areas of instinctual needs that every human being experiences in growing up. Jesus was tempted to satisfy his bodily hunger by seeking security in magic rather than in God; to jump off the pinnacle of the temple in order to make a name for himself as a wonder-worker; and to fall down and worship Satan in order to receive in exchange absolute power over the nations of the world. Security, esteem, power — these are three classic areas where temptation works on our false programs for happiness.

Genuine human growth incorporates all that is good on the more primitive levels of consciousness as one ascends to higher levels. Only the limitations of the earlier levels are left behind. For example, the need for security and survival, a biological necessity for the infant, has to be integrated with other values as the organism experiences the unfolding of its human potentialities. For a human being in whom the desire for security has never been moderated by reason, there is never enough security no matter how much wealth or power is accumulated. Similarly, one who has not integrated the desire for affection and esteem, in the face of one critical remark, may require a week's vacation with tranquilizers to recover from the blow.

Here is a parable from another tradition that might throw light on the meaning of repentance in the Christian perspective.

A Sufi master had lost the key to his house and was looking for it on the lawn outside, running his fingers through each blade of grass. His disciples came along and asked the master what had happened. "I have lost the key to my house," he said. "Can we help you find it?" they asked. "I'd be delighted!" he replied. With that the disciples got down on their hands and knees beside him and started running their fingers through the grass, too. After some hours, one of them asked, "Master, have you any idea where you might have lost the key?" He answered, "Yes, of course. I lost it in the house." The disciples looked at one another in astonishment. "Then why are we looking for it out here?" they exclaimed. The master replied, "Because there is more light here!"

This parable speaks to the human condition. We have all lost the key to happiness and are looking for it outside ourselves where it cannot possibly be found. We search outside because it is easier or more pleasant; there is more light there. There is also more company. If we look for happiness in emotional programs that promise happiness through symbols of security/survival, affection/esteem, or power/control, we can find plenty of help, because everyone else is trying to do the same thing. When we look for the key where it can be found, we may find ourselves alone, abandoned by friends and relatives who feel threatened by our search. Lack of support for the spiritual journey, not to mention positive opposition, is one of its heaviest trials.

When we decide to follow the call of Christ, we soon find our emotional programs for happiness in opposition to the value system of the Gospel which we have embraced. The false-self system, firmly in place from early childhood, does not drop dead upon request. Paul describes this experience poignantly when he writes,

> No matter which way I turn, I can't make myself do right. I want to, but I can't. When I want to do good, I don't; and when I try not to do wrong, I do it anyway. Now if I am doing what I don't want to, it is plain where the trouble is: sin still has me in its evil grasp. It seems to be a fact of life that when I want to do what is right, I inevitably do what is wrong. I love to do God's will, so far as my new nature is concerned; but there is something else deep within me, in my lower nature, that is at war with my mind and wins the fight, and makes me a slave

to the sin that is still within me. In my mind I want to be God's willing servant, but instead I find myself still enslaved to sin. My new life tells me to do right, but the old nature that is still inside me loves to sin. Oh, what a terrible predicament I am in! Who will free me from my slavery to this deadly lower nature? Thank God! It has been done by Jesus Christ the Lord. He has set me free.[2]

The struggle between the old and the new self is a constant theme in the New Testament. The false self easily adjusts to the circumstances of the spiritual journey as long as it does not have to change itself. Thus, it manifests its radical self-centeredness in various expressions of human activity: in material pursuits such as wealth and power; in emotional satisfactions such as relationships; in intellectual goals such as Ph.D.'s; in social goals such as status and prestige; in religious aspirations such as fasting and acts of piety; and even in spiritual commitments such as prayer, the practice of virtue and every form of ministry.

The Gospel calls us forth to full responsibility for our emotional life. We tend to blame other people or situations for the turmoil we experience. In actual fact, upsetting emotions prove beyond any doubt that the problem is in us. If we do not assume responsibility for our emotional programs on the unconscious level and take measures to change them, we will be influenced by them to the end of our lives. As long as these programs are in place, we cannot hear other people and their cries for help; their problems must first be filtered through our own emotional needs, reactions and prepackaged values. No amount of theological, scriptural or liturgical study can heal the false-self system, because as long as our emotional programs for happiness are firmly in place, such studies are easily co-opted by them.

The heart of the Christian ascesis — and the work of Lent — is to face the unconscious values that underlie the emotional programs for happiness and *to change them.* Hence the need of a discipline of contemplative prayer and action.

THE TEMPTATIONS IN THE DESERT

Jesus was led into the desert by the Spirit to be tempted by the devil. He fasted forty days and forty nights, and afterward was hungry. The tempter approached and said to him: "If you are the Son of God, command these stones to turn into bread."

Jesus replied, "Scripture has it, 'Not on bread alone is man to live, but on every utterance that comes from the mouth of God.' "

Next the devil took him to the holy city, set him upon the parapet of the temple, and said, "If you are the Son of God, throw yourself down. Scripture has it, 'He will bid his angels take care of you; with their hands they will support you that you may never stumble on a stone.' "

Jesus replied, "Scripture also has it, 'You shall not put the Lord your God to the test.' "

The devil then took him to a lofty mountain peak and displayed before him all the kingdoms of the world in their magnificence, promising, "All these will I bestow on you if you prostrate yourself in homage before me."

At this, Jesus said to him, "Away with you, Satan! Scripture says: 'You shall do homage to the Lord your God; him alone shall you adore.' "

At that the devil left him, and angels came and waited on him. [Matt. 4:1-11][3]

Lent is the season in which the church as a whole enters into an extended retreat. Jesus went into the desert for forty days and forty nights. The practice of Lent is a participation in Jesus' solitude, silence and privation.

The forty days of Lent bring into focus a long biblical tradition beginning with the Flood in the Book of Genesis, when rain fell upon the earth for forty days and forty nights. We read about Elijah walking forty days and forty nights to the mountain of God, Mt. Horeb. We read about the forty years that the Israelites wandered through the desert in order to reach the Promised Land. The biblical desert is primarily a place of purification, a place of passage. The biblical desert is not so much a geographical location — a place of sand, stones or sagebrush — as a process of interior purification leading to the complete liberation from the false-self system with its programs for happiness that cannot possibly work.

Jesus deliberately took upon himself the human condition — fragile, broken, alienated from God and other people. A whole program of self-centered concerns has been built up around our instinctual needs and have become energy centers — sources of motivation around which our emotions, thoughts and behavior patterns circulate like planets around the sun. Whether consciously or unconsciously, these programs for happiness influence our view of the world and our relationship with God, nature, other people and ourselves. This is the situation that Jesus went into the desert to heal. During Lent our work is to confront these programs for happiness and to detach ourselves from them. The scripture readings chosen for Lent and the example of Jesus encourage us in this struggle for inner freedom and conversion.

Jesus redeemed us from the consequences of our emotional programs for happiness by experiencing them himself. As a human being, he passed through the pre-rational stages of developing human consciousness: immersion in matter; the emergence of a body-self; and the development of conformity consciousness — over-identification with one's family, nation, ethnic group and religion. He had to deal with the particular but limited values of each level of human development from infancy to the age of reason, without, of course, ever ratifying with his will their illusory projects for happiness.

Jesus appears in the desert as the representative of the human race. He bears within himself the experience of the human predicament in its raw intensity. Hence, he is vulnerable to the temptations of Satan. Satan in the New Testament means the Enemy or the Adversary, a mysterious and malicious spirit that seems to be more than a mere personification of our unconscious evil tendencies. The temptations of Satan are allowed by God to help us confront our own evil tendencies. If relatives and friends fail to bring out the worst in us, Satan is always around to finish the job. Self-knowledge is experiential; it tastes the full depths of human weakness.

In the desert Jesus is tempted by the primitive instincts of human nature. Satan first addresses Jesus' security/survival needs, which constitute the first energy center: "If you are the Son of God, command these stones to become bread."

After fasting forty days and forty nights, Jesus must have been desperately hungry. His reply to Satan's suggestion is that it is not up to him to protect or to save himself; it is up to the Father to provide for him. "Not on bread alone does one live, but on every word that comes from the mouth of God." God has promised to provide for everyone who trusts in him. Jesus refuses to take his own salvation in hand and waits for God to rescue him.

The devil then took Jesus to the holy city, set him on the parapet of the temple and suggested, "If you are the Son of God, throw yourself down. Scripture has it, 'He will bid his angels take care of you; with their hands they will support you, that you may not stumble upon a stone!' "

In other words, "If you are the Son of God, manifest your power as a wonder-worker. Jump off this skyscraper. When you stand up and walk, everybody will regard you as a bigshot and bow down before you." This is the temptation to love fame and public esteem.

Affection/esteem constitute the center of gravity of the second energy center. Everybody needs a measure of acceptance and affirmation. In the path from infancy to adulthood, if these needs are denied, one seeks compensation for the real or imagined deprivations of early childhood. The greater the deprivation, the greater the neurotic drive for compensation.

In the text, Satan subtly quotes Psalm 90, the great theme song of Lent, a psalm of boundless confidence in God under all circumstances. He suggests that if Jesus leaps off the temple parapet, God will have to protect him. Jesus responds, "You shall not put the Lord your God to the test." In other words, no matter how many proofs of God's special love we may have, we may not take our salvation into our own hands. Jesus rejects the happiness program that seeks the glorification of the self as a wonder-worker or spiritual luminary.

The third energy center is the desire to control events and to have power over others. Satan took Jesus to a lofty mountain and displayed before him all the kingdoms of the world, promising, "All these I will bestow on you if you prostrate yourself in homage before me." The temptation to worship Satan in exchange for the symbols of unlimited power is the last-ditch effort of the false self to achieve its own invulnerability and immortality. Jesus replies, "Away with you, Satan. Scripture says, 'You shall do homage to the Lord your God; him alone shall you adore.'" Adoration of God is the antidote to pride and the lust for power. Service of others and not domination is the path to true happiness.

Thus, out of love for us, Jesus experienced the temptations of the first three energy centers. Each Lent he invites us to join him in the desert and to share his trials. The Lenten observances are designed to facilitate the reduction of our emotional investment in the programs of early childhood. Liberation from the entire false-self system is the ultimate purpose of Lent. This process always has Easter as its goal. The primary observance of Lent is to confront the false-self. Fasting, prayer and almsgiving are in the service of this project. As we dismantle our emotional programs for happiness, the obstacles to the risen life of Jesus fall away, and our hearts are prepared for the infusion of divine life at Easter.

THE TRANSFIGURATION

Jesus took Peter, James, and his brother John and led them up on a high mountain by themselves. He was transfigured before their eyes. His face became as dazzling as the sun, his clothes as radiant as light. Suddenly, Moses and Elijah appeared to them conversing with him. Upon this, Peter said, "Lord, how good it is for us to be here! With your permission, I will erect three booths here, one for you, one for Moses, and one for Elijah."

He was still speaking when suddenly a bright cloud overshadowed them. Out of the cloud came a voice which said, "This is my beloved Son on whom my favor rests. Listen to him."

When they heard this the disciples fell forward on the ground, overcome with fear. Jesus came toward them and laying his hand on them, said, "Get up! Do not be afraid." When they looked up they did not see anyone but Jesus. [Matt. 17:1-9][4]

On the first Sunday of Lent we were invited to accompany Jesus into the desert, there to confront the basic framework of the human condition: the emotional programs for happiness that develop around the instinctual needs of early childhood and eventually grow into energy centers. We continue to react, think, feel and act out of these centers of motivation unless we take ourselves in hand and try to change them. Jesus, being fully human, had the roots of these emotional programs in himself as he grew from infancy to manhood.

This text is the continuation of the invitation of Lent to undertake the inner purification that is required for divine union. On the mountain Jesus was "transfigured", that is to say, the divine Source of his human personality poured out through every pore of his body in the form of light. His face became dazzling as the sun. Even his clothes shared in the radiance of the inner glory that was flowing out through his body. By choosing this text for the second Sunday of Lent, the liturgy points to the fruit of struggling with the temptations arising from our conscious or unconscious emotional programming and of dying to the false-self system. Repentance leads to contemplation.

The Transfiguration manifests the kind of consciousness that Jesus enjoyed, which was not bound by the three-dimensional world. The spacious world of unity with the Ultimate Reality enabled him to be in direct contact with all creation, past, present and future.

The Transfiguration also reveals the state of mind and dispositions of the apostles who are paradigms of the developing consciousness of those who are growing in faith. In this experience, they are given a significant glimpse of the world beyond the limitations of space and time. At first they are overjoyed by the sensible consolation that floods their bodies and minds in the presence of the vision of Christ's glory. Then the implications of this new world with its demands dawns upon them, and they are terrified. At the end of the vision, they experienced the reassurance of Jesus' presence and touch. This presence vastly surpassed the ephemeral sweetness of their initial taste of sensible consolation. Their exterior and interior senses were quieted by the awesomeness of the Mystery manifested by the voice out of the cloud. Once their senses had been calmed and integrated into the spiritual experience which their intuitive faculties had perceived, peace was established throughout their whole being, and they were prepared to respond to the guidance of the Spirit.

Notice the influence of the false-self system at work in Peter. He was overwhelmed by the light emerging from the presence of Jesus. Like the other apostles, his senses were delighted. He saw the wonder of Moses and Elijah appearing and talking with Jesus. Both prophets had experienced forty days of purification, one on Mt. Sinai, the other on his long trek to Mt. Horeb. In the spiritual world there are no barriers of time or space; everyone is interrelated.

Peter's reaction to the vision was, "This is great! Let's make it permanent. Let us make three booths: one for Jesus, one for Moses and one for Elijah." Although this suggestion was very hospitable, it was singularly inappropriate. As was his custom, Peter moves to center-stage. Without being invited, he takes charge of the situation: "Let's build three booths."

Suddenly a cloud overshadowed Jesus, the prophets and the three apostles. It silenced Peter. A voice said, "This is my beloved. Listen to him." The apostles fell forward on their faces in an attitude of awe, praise, gratitude and love, all rolled into one.

The apostles remained in this position until Jesus touched them. "Don't be afraid," he said. They looked up and saw no one but Jesus. The experience of God may be scary at first but quickly becomes reassuring. Actually, there is nothing to be afraid of because we were made for divine union.

Here we find the basic pattern of the Christian path. Jesus, by his example and teaching, approaches us from without in order to awaken us to his divine Presence within. The Eternal Word of God has always been speaking to us interiorly, but we have not been able to hear his voice. When we are adequately prepared, the interior Word begins to be heard. The external word of scripture and the interior Word arising from the depths of our being become one. Our inner experience is confirmed by what we hear in the liturgy and read in scripture.

The ideal disposition for the divine encounter is the gathering together of one's whole being in silent and alert attentiveness. The practice of interior silence produces gradually what the voice in the vision produced instantly: the capacity to listen. It withdraws the false self from its self-centeredness and allows the true self to emerge into our awareness.

Revelation, in the fullest sense of the term, is our personal awakening to Christ. The external word of God and the liturgy dispose us for the experience of Christ's risen life within us. It is to this that the spiritual exercises of Lent are ordered. The awakening to the divine Presence emerges from what Meister Eckhardt called "the ground of being" — that level of being which in Christ is divine by nature and which in us is divine by participation.

THE PRODIGAL SON

The tax collectors and the sinners were all gathering around Jesus to hear him, at which the Pharisees and the scribes murmured, "This man welcomes sinners and eats with them." Then he addressed this parable to them:

A man had two sons. The younger of them said to his father, "Father, give me the share of the estate that is coming to me." So the father divided up the property. Some days later this younger son collected all his belongings and went off to a distant land, where he squandered his money on dissolute living. After he had spent everything, a great famine broke out in that country and he was in dire need. So he attached himself to one of the propertied class of the place, who sent him to his farm to take care of the pigs. He longed to fill his belly with the husks that were fodder for the pigs, but no one made a move to give him anything.

Coming to his senses at last, he said: "How many hired hands at my father's place have more than enough to eat, while here

I am starving! I will break away and return to my father, and say to him, 'Father, I have sinned against God and against you; I no longer deserve to be called your son. Treat me like one of your hired hands.'" With that he set off for his father's house.

While he was still a long way off, his father caught sight of him and was deeply moved. He ran out to meet him, threw his arms around his neck, and kissed him. The son said to him, "Father, I have sinned against God and against you; I no longer deserve to be called your son."

The father said to his servants: "Quick, bring out the finest robe and put it on him; put a ring on his finger and shoes on his feet. Take the fatted calf and kill it. Let us eat and celebrate because this son of mine was dead and has come back to life. He was lost and is found." Then the celebration began.

Meanwhile, the elder son was out on the land. As he neared the house on his way home, he heard the sound of music and dancing. He called one of the servants and asked him the reason for the dancing and the music. The servant answered, "Your brother is home, and your father has killed the fatted calf because he has him back in good health." The son grew angry at this and would not go in; but his father came out and began to plead with him.

He said in reply to his father: "For years now I have slaved for you. I never disobeyed one of our orders, yet you never gave me so much as a kid goat to celebrate with my friends. Then, when this son of yours returns after having gone through your property with loose women, you kill the fatted calf for him."

"My son," replied the father, "you are with me always, and everything I have is yours. But we had to celebrate and rejoice! This brother of yours was dead, and has come to life. He was lost, and is found." [Luke 15:1-32][5]

To understand the main thrust of this remarkable parable, it is good to remember to whom it was addressed. The public sinners had gathered to listen to Jesus to see what he might have to say, to check him out. Some of the scribes and pharisees were also present. They complained that he hobnobbed and hung out with tax collectors and prostitutes. Tax collecting was considered the lowest form of earning a living at that time. Jesus presents us with an image of God that must have come as quite a shock to everybody. Jesus spoke of Yahweh as "*Abba*", Father, the God of infinite compassion.

This was a revolutionary way of speaking of God compared to the popular concept of Yahweh as the God of armies.

The father in this parable was well-to-do and had two sons. The younger one seems to have had no sense at all. He was interested in his share of the inheritance because he wanted to live it up before he got too old, and this would cost money. So he negotiated with his father to hand over whatever was coming to him. He did not say what he was going to do with the money and his father did not inquire; he preferred to trust his son who was now a man. It only took the young man about three days after he got his hands on the money to pack his belongings and to take off to see the world. He went into a far country where nobody could check up on him and where he could have the maximum freedom to do what he liked. His luxurious living quickly consumed the fortune. The inheritance, of course, was not something that was owed to him, but something someone else had worked for; he just happened to be the heir.

The younger son was not a good manager. He drank a lot, caroused and squandered the money. Then what happened? As generally happens with projects for sheer pleasure, his plans did not work out as expected. He got clobbered by circumstances. This is the only way for some people to learn that their emotional projects for happiness are, in fact, programs for human misery. They go bankrupt, suffer a painful divorce, lose a child in an accident, are rejected by the people they most love, become alcoholics or drug addicts, and wind up on skid row or in a mental hospital. There it finally dawns on them that their happiness projects are not working out as well as expected.

In similar fashion, the only way that this young man discovered his mistake was to encounter disaster. A famine broke out in the country where he was living. Soon he was starving and the only job he could get was tending a herd of swine. But no one even offered him the husks that the swine were eating to assuage his hunger. In the popular opinion of his milieu, nothing could be worse than taking care of pigs. The young man had hit bottom. He began to reflect on the situation of the hired hands at home. Even if they did not have a share in the inheritance, they were well-fed. It was hard to leave the land of his cherished dreams of unlimited pleasure, but now all his fantasies had been shattered by the famine, his shameful occupation and his aching hunger. Reality, as it always does, had significantly insinuated itself into his emotional projects for happiness.

He decided to return to his father and began the long journey home.

As he went, he prepared a speech to present to his father. "Father, I have sinned against God and against you; I no longer deserve to be called your son. Treat me as one of your hired hands."

As he neared the paternal estate, his father caught sight of him a long way off. The bereaved father had evidently been on the lookout for his long-lost son. As soon as he spotted him, he ran down the road to greet him, threw his arms around him and kissed him. The young man started to recite the speech he had so carefully prepared, but his father did not wait for him to finish. The Prodigal only got as far as to say that he was unworthy to be called his son. He never got the chance to say, "Treat me as one of your hired hands," because his father was too busy kissing and embracing him.

The father immediately calls his servants to bring out the finest robe, a precious ring, sandals for his son's bleeding feet, and to prepare the fatted calf, symbol of the epitome of celebration. The party begins. There is dancing, music, and everybody is having a bash. The father is aglow with happiness and the Prodigal is beginning to regain a glimmer of renewed self-respect. Everything is as it was before his departure, only more so.

This first part of the story is clearly addressed to the tax collectors, public sinners and prostitutes who happened to be listening. We next hear about the Elder Son who was working in the fields. He hears the celebration going on and asks one of the servants, "What is this rejoicing all about?" When he learns that his ne'er-do-well brother, who went off with half of the inheritance and squandered it, is the cause of the celebration, he is fit to be tied. He stoutly refuses to go in to the party. His father hears about this and comes out to remonstrate with him. The Elder Son refuses to listen and blasts the old man with an outburst marked by harshness toward his brother and bitterness toward his father. "This is unjust," he complains. "This guy wasted the inheritance you worked so hard to acquire. I have slaved for you all my life, and you never gave me so much as a kid goat to celebrate with my friends!"

His father replies, "Son, everything I have is yours. But we had to celebrate and rejoice. This brother of yours was dead, and has come back to life."

The story ends without our knowing whether the Elder Son came in and joined the celebration. But this much is certain. The parable is not just about the Prodigal Son. It is about two prodigal sons. The elder brother turns out to be a bigger sinner than the younger. He is the chief prodigal because he refuses to forgive. He is just as interested in the inheritance, or more so, than the younger son who squandered it on a good time. The inheritance was a symbol for him of prestige, security and power. He thought that he could guarantee his share by earning it. But salvation, the sublime inheritance that is the central point of this parable, cannot be earned; it can only be received. The divine inheritance is the banquet of the Father's love. The Prodigal Son accepted the invitation to the banquet. The Elder Son refused. He did not understand that the divine inheritance consists in participating in the Father's love, a love whose only condition is that we accept it as a gift. The younger son came to understand the futility of his self-centered projects for happiness through disaster. The elder was favored by the quiet call to growth contained in the faithful fulfillment of his duties as eldest son. Unfortunately, his self-centered projects for happiness prevented him from recognizing the precious gift he was being offered. Thus he squandered his inheritance just as much as his younger brother.

This parable does not stop at upsetting the prevailing value systems of the time. The self-righteous pharisees felt that the special favor of God belonged to them in view of their good works. From that vantage point, it was easy to despise those who indulged in the weaknesses of human nature. This is the typical attitude of people who serve God for the sake of reward. As a result of their service, they feel that they have a strict right to suitable remuneration. The pharisees complained when Jesus offered God's forgiveness to publicans and sinners. The parable, as Jesus' response to their complaints, implies that sinners rejected by society are more apt than they are to receive the reign of God. Unlike the pharisees, public sinners do not have the attitude that God owes them something. The scribes and pharisees had kept all the commandments except the most important one, which was to show love.

The parable invites us to consider our own value system. Lent is about repentance, about letting go of our false value system in order to open to the values of the Gospel. The chief point of this parable is the invitation to each of us (whichever son you wish to identify with) to recognize that the reign of God is sheer gift. The divine inheritance does not belong to us or anyone else. It is the result of the sheer goodness of our Father. The father in this parable is characterized by unconditional love toward both his sons, each of whom abused the inheritance by wanting to take possession of it in his own way. Each is equally guilty of rejecting the goodness and love of this extraordinary father who is not put off by either of them; neither by the wild dissipation of the younger son, nor by the bitter self-righteousness of the elder. The Elder Son is offered just as much mercy as the younger, but because of his self-righteousness, it is harder for him to receive it. His pride will not allow him to accept the inheritance as sheer gift.

Actually, there is no inheritance; there is only stewardship for what has been freely given. As stewards, we have an obligation to share with others the mercy we have freely received. This is the value system that shook the conventional piety of the people of Jesus' time to its roots.

MARTHA AND MARY

> Now as they went on their way, he entered a village; and a woman named Martha received him into her house. And she had a sister called Mary who sat at the Lord's feet and listened to his teaching. But Martha was distracted with much serving; and she went to him and said, "Lord, do you not care that my sister has left me to serve alone? Telle her then to help me." But the Lord answered her, "Martha, Martha, you are anxious and troubled about many things; one thing is needful. Mary has chosen the good portion, which shall not be taken away from her." [Luke 10:38-42]

This text is one that has exercised exegetes down through the ages and has been the basis for distinguishing two evangelical lifestyles, the contemplative and the active. On closer look, however, the point of this story is not about which lifestyle is more perfect, but about the quality of Christian life. What Jesus disapproves of in Martha's behavior is not her good works, of which he was about to be the beneficiary, but her motive in doing them. The quality of one's service does not come from the activity itself, but from the purity of one's intention. The single eye of the Gospel is the eye of love, which is the desire to please God in all our actions, whatever these may be. Jesus' defense of Mary, who was sitting at his feet, is not an excuse for lazy folks to avoid the chores. But neither is it a motive for those who are working hard to get annoyed if those engaged in a contemplative lifestyle do not come forth to help them.

The story is a parable about the quality of Christian life, about growing in it, and about the necessity of the contemplative dimension of the Gospel as the means of doing so. When Jesus tells Martha that Mary had chosen the good portion, he is telling Martha that she needs to find a place in her life for this contemplative quality, and that this perspective would make her good actions better. He is also warning Mary that there is something even better than the good portion. This is the union of contemplation and action.

Purity of intention developed through contemplation brings to action the quality of love. Without contemplative prayer, action easily becomes mechanical, routine, draining, and may lead to burnout. At the very least, it fails to perceive the goldmine that ordinary life contains. Daily life is practice number-one for a Christian, but it can cease to be a practice without the discipline of contemplative prayer. The contemplative dimension of the Gospel perceives in daily life the treasures of holiness hidden in the most trivial and mundane events.

Jesus' statement is a call both to Mary and Martha, not just to Martha. Martha's activity was good, Mary's was better, but neither was good enough. Both needed to move into the union and harmony of the two, which is the contemplative dimension of the Gospel. Through contemplative prayer we come under the influence of the Spirit both in prayer and action. Then action is truly prayer. Prayer is relationship, and hence capable of almost infinite growth. Relationship can go on growing forever, especially relationship with the infinite God. Prayer is the relationship in which purity of heart, reached through the unloading of the unconscious and the dismantling of the false-self system, opens us to the will of God in everything and enables us to respond out of divine love to the events of everyday life.

Jesus said to Martha, "You are agitated and upset by many things." "Agitated" is the key word; it means that she was attached to her activity, or possibly to Mary's inactivity. She was serving the Lord to please herself, not with purity of heart, which seeks to please God and to do what divine love would do in each situation. Her agitation pointed to the fact that one of her emotional programs for happiness had been frustrated. There was nothing wrong with her activity, but to be agitated or upset indicated that she was under the influence of the false self and withdrawn from the purity of divine inspiration.

This parable encourages us to seek the integration of action and prayer. The time of contemplative prayer is the place of encounter between the creative vision of union with Christ and its incarnation in daily life. Without this daily confrontation, the contemplative vision can stagnate into a privatized game of perfectionism or succumb to the subtle poison of seeking one's own satisfaction in prayer. On the other hand, without the contemplative vision, daily renewed in contemplative prayer, action can become self-centered and forgetful of God. The contemplative dimension guarantees the union of Martha and Mary. This union is symbolized by Lazarus, who was the third member of the household. He is the symbol of the union of the active and contemplative lives. The mysterious illness that led to his death was self-knowledge, the awareness of his false-self system. As the risen life of Christ emerges from the ashes of his false-self system, he enters into the freedom and joy of divine life.

Teresa of Avila says that transforming union might be likened to the transformation of a worm into a butterfly. The life of a butterfly totally transcends that of a worm, but the worm contributes to the process by weaving its own cocoon. By the regular practice of contemplative prayer and by dismantling the emotional programs for happiness, we too weave our cocoon, die to the false-self system, and await the moment of resurrection.

THE ANOINTING AT BETHANY

Six days before the Passover Jesus was in the home of Simon the leper at Bethany. While he reclined at table, a woman with an alabaster flask of pure and very costly nard perfume entered the room. She broke the alabaster flask and emptied it over his head.

Now some were indignant, saying to one another: "What good is the waste of this perfume: Why, this perfume could have been sold for upwards of three-hundred denarii and the money given to the poor!" So they gave way to bitter feelings toward her.

But Jesus said, "Let her have her way. Why do you molest her? She has given beautiful expression of her devotion to me. After all, you always have the poor with you, but you do not always have me. She did what she could: by anointing my body, she prepared it for burial just in time! I assure you, wherever the Gospel is preached, in any part of the world, what this woman has done will likewise be proclaimed to perpetuate her memory." [Mark 14:3-9][6]

This Gospel must be of great importance. Wherever the good news is preached, this event is to be repeated, so that everyone will know of this woman's devotion to Jesus. She is identified in John's Gospel as Mary of Bethany. John records the setting of this event in the following words: "Six days before the Passover Jesus came to Bethany." The home of Lazarus, Martha and Mary was a favorite stopping-off place for Jesus on his trips to Jerusalem.

Mary of Bethany is one of the few persons in the Gospel who are clearly delineated. As we saw in the last chapter, she was a contemplative. She is depicted as sitting at the feet of Jesus and listening to him — the principal practice of contemplative prayer. The Gospel says she was listening to his word, not his words. She was not following his teaching at this point. She was listening to him, that is, to the Speaker. She was identifying with the divine Person of the Word beyond his human words. She was moving to deeper levels of identification with him, beyond thinking, feeling and particular acts. She magnificently exemplifies what contemplative prayer is: the interiorization of the *person* of Jesus Christ, not just his words and teaching.

Evidently this meant a lot to Jesus because he would not allow her to be disturbed by her sister's importunities. Few people have ever been defended in this manner by divine Wisdom itself. It was in answer to her prayer that Jesus had raised Lazarus from the dead a few days before.

The dinner at Bethany was given in honor of Jesus six days before his passion and death. The Jewish authorities were now plotting vigorously for his destruction. Judas had already decided to betray him into the hands of his enemies. Simon the leper was the host at the dinner. Martha was fulfilling her customary role as perfect hostess, and Lazarus was one of the guests at table. It was an interesting group of people: Jesus the Messiah, Mary the contemplative, Martha the activist, Simon the leper, Judas the thief, and Lazarus the corpse — a fairly motley crew — what we might call a typical Sunday congregation. Jesus does not always choose the most respectable people to be his guests.

Everyone was reclining at table except Mary. When she walked in, all eyes turned toward her. Everybody knew she had a deep love for Jesus. She was carrying an alabaster jar in which there was a pound of nard perfume. A pound of nard perfume was extremely expensive. Later we learn that it was worth three-hundred denarii, an amount that represented the ordinary workingman's wages for an entire year.

She entered the room carrying the alabaster jar filled to the brim with the precious nard perfume and came to where Jesus was reclining. Suddenly, without a word, she smashed the bottle and poured the entire contents over his head. Out poured a pound of the incredibly costly perfume. The delicious odor billowed forth, filling the whole house with its fragrance. John adds that Mary also anointed the feet of Jesus and wiped them with her hair.

The guests were flabbergasted. No one had ever done anything like this. Was the woman crazy? Gradually, the disciples regained their composure and started grumbling. They said to one another, "Why wasn't this costly perfume sold and the proceeds given to the poor? What a waste!"

John identifies Judas as the ringleader of these remarks and comments sardonically, "It was not because he loved the poor that he said this, but because he was a thief and used to take what was put in the common purse and put it in his own pocket." The other disciples, however, also gave way to bitter feelings against her.

Jesus then intervened with the words, "Let her have her way." He was dripping with perfume from head to foot, saturated with the stuff, a whole pound of it!

When a well-to-do lady is invited to an important dinner and wants to put her best foot forward, she may dab a little perfume on her hair. But how much would she use? Probably just a tiny bit. What would she think if her husband came in and said, "Darling, I want you to smell nice," and poured a pound of the most expensive perfume on the market over her head?

The house was now filled with a dense cloud of delicious perfume billowing through every room. The scent was overpowering. The disciples continued to complain. Nobody could eat; the meal had come to an end. Mary's astonishing action had completely shattered the festive atmosphere. Everyone was upset except Jesus.

"Why do you bother her?" he continued. "She has given a beautiful expression of her devotion to me." The Master had perceived the meaning of Mary's symbolic gesture. She had penetrated the Mystery of Jesus' true identity far in advance of the disciples.

In the cultural context of the time, courtesy required anointing the head of an honored guest with oil, washing his feet and giving him a kiss. These were the ordinary courtesies extended to everyone invited to an important dinner. The crucial point that Mary was trying to express by means of her symbolic gesture was, "This is no ordinary guest! The ordinary courtesies are not enough!"

Mary was aware of what was being plotted by the authorities and wanted to affirm the depth of her faith in Jesus in a way that could not possibly be misunderstood. Some gesture had to be made before it was too late. Everyone recognized that by anointing him with expensive perfume, the symbol of her love, she was expressing her devotion to him and manifesting the gift of herself. But the deepest meaning of her symbolic gesture was not simply the gift of herself, but the *totality* of that gift. Not only did she anoint him with the costly perfume; she smashed the bottle and emptied its entire contents over his head! She threw herself away, so to speak, emptying every last drop of the perfume in superabundant expression of the *total* gift of herself. This is the meaning of her extraordinary gesture as Jesus perceived it and which so moved him. "You always have the poor with you," he said, "but you do not always have me. She did what she could: by anointing my body, she prepared it for burial just in time."

Anointing the bodies of the dead was one of the burial rites of the Jews at the time of Jesus. By referring to this practice, Jesus introduces a further element in her extraordinary gesture. The smashing of the jar filled with precious perfume represents not only Mary's total gift of herself to Christ; it also represents the totality of the Father's gift to us in Christ. Her action prefigures the smashing of Jesus' body on the cross. His body is the alabaster jar filled with the perfume of infinite value, that is, the Spirit of God. It was to be broken to pieces in order that the divine Spirit dwelling in it might be poured out over the world without any limit and fill the entire human family with divine love.

Mary's prophetic action points to the crushing of Jesus' body on the cross as the symbol of the Father's infinite mercy, the visible sign of God's fundamental attitude toward the human family: unconditional love. In the passion of Jesus, God throws himself away, so to speak, and dies for us.

In this remarkable incident, Mary manifests her intuition into what Jesus is about to do. Moreover, she identifies with him to such an intimate degree that she manifests the same disposition of total self-giving that he is about to manifest on the cross. She had learned from Jesus how to throw herself away and become like God. That is why this story must be proclaimed wherever the Gospel is preached. "To perpetuate Mary's memory" is to fill the whole world with the perfume of God's love, the love that is totally self-giving. In the concrete, it is to anoint the poor and the afflicted, the favored members of Christ's Body, with this love.

THE FATHER AND I ARE ONE

Jesus said to his disciples: "Do not let your hearts be troubled. Have faith in God and faith in me. In my Father's house there are many dwelling places; otherwise, how could I have told you that I was going to prepare a place for you? I am indeed going to prepare a place for you, and then I shall come back to take you with me, that where I am you also may be. You know the way that leads where I go."

"Lord," said Thomas, "we do not know where you are going. How can we know the way?" Jesus told him: "I am the way, and the truth, and the life; no one comes to the Father but through me. If you really knew me, you would know my Father also. From this point on you know him; you have seen him."

"Lord," Philip said to him, "show us the Father and that will be enough for us." "Philip," Jesus replied, "after I have been with you all this time, you still do not know me?"

"Whoever has seen me has seen the Father. How can you say, 'Show us the Father'? Do you not believe that I am in the Father and the Father is in me? The words I speak are not spoken of myself; it is the Father who lives in me accomplishing his works. Believe me that I am in the Father and the Father is in me, or else, believe because of the works I do. I solemnly assure you, the one who has faith in me will do the works I do, and greater far than these. Why? Because I go to the Father." [John 14:1-12][7]

The basic text for Christian practice is "the Father and I are one."[8] Christ came to save us from our sins, but only as the essential preliminary to our ultimate destiny. The source of all sin is the sense of a separate self. The separate-self sense is, of course, the false self, but not only the false-self, as we shall see. The false self is to be surrendered to Christ through the love of his sacred humanity and the divine Person who possesses it. Christ is the way to the Father. His human nature and personality is the door to his divinity. By identification with him as a human being, we find our true self — the divine life within us — and begin the process of integration into the life of the Father, Son and Holy Spirit.

Christ came to communicate to each of us his own personal experience of the Father. However, even when the separate self has been joined to

Christ, it is still a self. The ultimate state to which we are called is beyond any fixed point of reference such as a self. It transcends the personal union with Christ to which Paul referred when he said, "It is no longer I who live, but Christ lives in me."[9]

The death of Jesus on the cross was the death of his personal self, which in his case was a deified self. Christ's resurrection and ascension is his passage into the Ultimate Reality: the sacrifice and loss of his deified self to become one with the Godhead. Since all reality is the manifestation of the Godhead and Christ has passed into identification with It, Christ is present everywhere and in everything. The cosmos is now the Body of the glorified Christ who dwells in every part of it.

Union with Christ on the cross — our entrance into his experience — leads to the death of our separate-self sense. To embrace the cross of Christ is to be willing to leave behind the self as a fixed point of reference. It is to die to all separation, even to a self that has been transformed. It is to be one with God, not just to experience it.

Jesus' invitation to "take up your cross every day and follow me" is a call to do what he actually did. As the Way, Jesus invites us to follow his example step-by-step into the bosom of the Father. As the Truth, he shares with us, through participation in his death on the cross, the experience of the transpersonal aspect of the Father. As the Life, he leads us to unity with the Godhead beyond personal and impersonal relationships. On the Christian path, God is known first as the personal God, then as the transpersonal God, and finally as the Ultimate Reality beyond all personal and impersonal categories. Since God's existence, knowledge and activity are one — Ultimate Reality is discovered to be *That-Which-Is*.

THE PASSION

> When they brought Jesus to Golgotha (which means the place of the skull), they tried to give him wine drugged with myrrh, but he would not take it. Then they crucified him and divided up his garments by rolling dice for them to see what each should take. It was about nine in the morning when they crucified him. . . .
>
> With him they crucified two insurgents, one at his right and one at his left. People going by kept insulting him, tossing

their heads and saying, "Ha, ha! So you were going to destroy the temple and rebuild it in three days! Save yourself now by coming down from that cross!"

The chief priests and the scribes also joined in and jeered, "He saved others, but he cannot save himself! Let the 'Messiah', the king of Israel, come down from the cross here and now so that we can see it and believe in him!" The men who had been crucified with him likewise kept taunting him.

When noon came, darkness fell on the whole countryside and lasted until midafternoon. At that time Jesus cried out in a loud voice, "Eloi, Eloi, lama sabachthani?" which means, "My God, my God, why have you forsaken me?"

A few of the bystanders who heard it remarked:"Listen! He is calling on Elijah." Someone ran, and soaking a sponge in sour wine, stuck it on a reed to try to make him drink. The man said, "Now let's see whether Elijah comes to take him down."

Then Jesus, uttering a loud cry, breathed his last. [Mark 15:22-38][10]

The double-bind is one of the crucial experiences of the spiritual journey. No one ever experienced it to the degree that Jesus did. By "double-bind" I mean a crisis of principle that brings about an overwhelming problem of conscience. Two apparent duties that call out for total adherence seem to be in complete opposition to each other. This is not the same as hitting bottom where there is no place to go but up. It is the agonizing problem of facing two opposing goods that cannot be integrated or resolved. Our dilemma is not a choice between good or evil, which would be a temptation. It is usually a choice between two apparent goods. Or again, an event may arise in our life that is absolutely contrary to our deepest loyalties, to our spiritual tradition, religious education or cultural conditioning. Such a choice or event causes incredible suffering, especially to those who are most advanced in purity of conscience. For a crisis of this kind there is no solution on the rational level. The double-bind can only be resolved by moving to a higher level of conscious-ness, where the two opposites that seem irreconcilable on the level of reason are resolved, not by rational explanation, but in the light of the new perspective that sees the opposites as complementary rather than contradictory.

One of the classical examples of this kind of crisis appears in the book of Job, one of the great wisdom books of the Old Testament. Through most of the book, Job is struggling with the problem of innocent suffering.

He knows himself to be innocent and yet he is experiencing tremendous suffering on every level of his being. He ends up sitting on a dunghill, covered with sores from head to foot. All his possessions, his family and friends have been taken from him, and he is overwhelmed by physical infirmities. Yet he had never offended God in any way. Prior to his misfortunes, he was recognized by everyone as a just man. His comforters, representing the cultural preconceptions of the time, kept telling him, "If only you will admit that you have sinned, God will forgive you and your suffering will be taken away."

In Job's day misfortune was considered a sign of personal sin; either one had done something wrong in early life, or one had committed a hidden sin. Job was confronted with the dilemma of being faithful to his own integrity (He knew he had not done anything wrong.) or of accusing God of injustice for allowing him to suffer as if he had committed some secret crime. Job maintains his innocence throughout the book. His double-bind consisted of trying to avoid accusing God of injustice and at the same time, of remaining faithful to his conscience which told him that he had done nothing wrong.

The resolution of Job's double-bind comes in the last chapter of the book, when God reveals to him a higher view of reality without explaining the mystery of innocent suffering. God seems to say that suffering is one of the impenetrables of life while remaining an inescapable part of it.

Job's suffering helps us understand what the passion of Jesus involved as a double-bind. In the desert Jesus experienced the human condition with the same concreteness with which we experience it, namely, in the form of the emotional programming of early childhood. As Jesus' life unfolded, his awareness of his personal union with the Father constantly increased. As he approached the end of his life, he revealed the God of Israel, not as a God of armies, of fear or of sheer transcendence, but as the God of compassion, a Presence that bends over creatures with incredible tenderness, care and affection. At the same time, God is firm in training his children so that they may grow into the transcendent destiny that he has planned for them.

No one ever knew God the way that Jesus knew him. He penetrated the depths of the Ultimate Reality and revealed that the interior life of Limitless Being is relationship: a community of persons sharing infinite life and love. Jesus entered into that relationship, made it his own, and tried to transmit it to his disciples. For him, the Father, *Abba,* was absolutely everything. In coming to the age of reason and to full reflective self-consciousness, Jesus never suffered from the feeling of separation from God that is our experience as we come to rational consciousness. This feeling of separation is the source of our deep sense of incompletion, guilt and alienation.

Jesus took upon himself the human condition more and more concretely as his life progressed. In the Garden of Gethsemani, he took upon himself the sin of the world with all its consequences. He experienced every level of loneliness, guilt and anguish that you or I or any human being has ever felt. The ghastly sum of accumulated human misery, sin and guilt descended upon him. He felt himself being asked by his Father to identify with this misery in all its immensity and horror. This was the double-bind Jesus articulates so graphically in the Garden of Gethsemani. After pleading in vain to the apostles to watch one hour with him, he withdrew a little way from them and fell on his face crying out, "Abba, if it be possible, let this chalice pass from me!" The clear realization that he was being asked by the Father to thrust himself as far from him as anyone has ever experienced, caused him unimaginable agony. By absorbing the separate-self sense into his inmost being, Jesus *became* sin. As Paul writes, "He who knew not sin was made sin for our salvation."

Jesus was torn between the choices presented by the double-bind: "Am I to become sin and thus renounce my personal relationship with Abba?" Or again, "Am I to become sin and thus experience separation from the One who is my whole life?"

His prayer continues, "Nevertheless, Father, not my will, but thine be done."

Jesus made this petition three times over and as he prayed, he sweat drops of blood, manifesting the incredible agony of his double-bind. The source of Jesus' dread was not so much the prospect of physical suffering, but the impending loss of his personal relationship with the One who meant everything to him.

"Father, how can I, your *Son*, become sin?" That is the cup of bitterness that Jesus desperately wanted to avoid. And yet, because of his boundless love for the Father and for us, he kept repeating with ever-increasing desperation, "Not my will, but Thine be done!"

"My Father, if it is possible, let this cup pass from me."[11] That is the voice of human weakness reaching to infinity, the voice of human sinfulness that Jesus took upon himself and identified with in the Garden.

"Not my will, but Thine be done." That is the voice of God's infinite love for us, throbbing in the heart of Christ, forgiving everything and everyone. Infinite weakness and infinite love have met in the passion and death of Jesus. Our anguish has become his anguish.

Jesus rose from his prayer and returned to the disciples only to find them asleep. There was to be no human support for him in his supreme moment of isolation and need. Soon all but one of the apostles would run away. Soon he was to be rejected by his own people, condemned by the civil and religious authorities, subjected to insult and mockery, and crucified between two murderers. In his last moments he would watch his life's work disintegrate before his eyes.

As Jesus approached the end of his physical endurance on the cross, he cried out, "My God, my God, why have you forsaken me?" With these words, he revealed the fact that the act of taking upon himself the entire weight of human sinfulness had cost him the loss of his personal union with the Father. It is the final stage of Jesus' spiritual journey. This double-bind, when it was resolved at the moment of his resurrection, catapulted him into a state of being beyond the personal union with the Father which had been his whole life until then. While his sacrifice opened up for the whole human family the possibility of sharing in his experience of personal union with the Father, it opened up for him a totally new level of being. His humanity was glorified to such a degree that he could enter the heart of all creation as its Source. Now he is present everywhere, in the inmost being of all creation, transcending time and space and bringing the transmission of divine life to its ultimate fulfillment.

Unity with the Godhead was the resolution of Jesus' double-bind. There is a resolution for every double-bind. It remains, however, a terrible crisis. In the face of such a crisis, one may regress to a lower level of consciousness. But one who seeks God will not give in to this temptation. The energy built up by living with the seemingly impossible situation will eventually give birth to the resolution that only God knows and that only God can give.

FATHER, HOW CAN I, YOUR SON, BECOME SIN?

> Your attitude must be Christ's:
> though he was in the form of God
> he did not deem equality with God
> something to be grasped at.
> Rather, he emptied himself

and took the form of a slave,
being born in the likeness of men.
He was known to be of human estate,
and it was thus he humbled himself,
obediently accepting even death,
death on a cross! Phil. 2:6-9

To become sin is to cease to be God's son — or at least to cease to be conscious of being God's son. To cease to be conscious of being God's son is to cease to experience God as Father. The cross of Jesus represents the ultimate death-of-God experience: "My God, my God, why have You forsaken me?" The crucifixion is much more than the physical death of Jesus and the emotional and mental anguish that accompanied it. It is the death of his human *self.* The crucifixion was not the death of his false self because he never had one. It was the death of his deified self and the annihilation of the ineffable union which he enjoyed with the Father in his human faculties. This was more than spiritual death; it was dying to being God and hence the dying *of* God: "He emptied himself, and took the form of a slave... accepting even death, death on a cross!" The loss of personal identity is the ultimate kenosis.

In the crucifixion, his human self disappeared and with it the loss of his experience of *who* God is. In his resurrection and ascension, Jesus discovered *what* God is, and in doing so, became one with Ultimate Reality: *what God is* emerging eternally from *what God is.*

This passing of Jesus from human to divine subjectivity is called in Christian tradition the *Paschal Mystery.* Our participation in this Mystery is the passing over of the transformed self into the experience of no-self[12]; of *who* God is into *what* God is. The dismantling of the false self and the inward journey to the true self is the first phase of this transition or passing over. The loss of the true self and the experience of no-self is the second phase. The first phase results in the consciousness of personal union with the Trinity. The second phase consists in being emptied of this union and identifying with the absolute nothingness from which all things emerge, to which all things return, and which manifests Itself as *That-Which-Is.*

THE BURIAL

It was now around midday, and darkness came over the whole land until midafternoon. . .Jesus uttered a loud cry and said, "Father, into your hands I commend my spirit." After he said this, he expired.

The centurion, upon seeing what had happened, gave glory to God by saying, "Surely this was an innocent man." After the crowd assembled for this spectacle witnessed what had happened, they returned beating their breasts. All his friends and the women who had accompanied him from Galilee were standing at a distance watching everything.

There was a man named Joseph . . . from Arimathea . . . and he looked expectantly for the reign of God. This man approached Pilate with a request for Jesus' body. He took it down, wrapped it in fine linen, and laid it in a tomb hewn out of rock, in which no one had yet been buried.

That was the day of Preparation, and the Sabbath was about to begin. The women who had come with him from Galilee followed along behind. They saw the tomb and how his body was buried. Then they went back home to prepare spices and perfumes. They observed the Sabbath as a day of rest, in accordance with the Law. [Luke 23:44-56][13]

Jesus died on the day before the Sabbath. His body was taken down in a hurry and laid in the tomb. The Sabbath commemorates the seventh day of creation, the day God rested from all his works. In honor of creation and at God's express command, the Jewish people observed the Sabbath as a day of complete rest. But its most profound meaning is contained in this particular Sabbath in which, having laid down his life for the human family, Jesus, the Son of God, rested.

Out of respect for the death of the Redeemer, there is no liturgical celebration on Holy Saturday. In honor of Jesus' body resting in the tomb, the church also rests. There is nothing more to be said, nothing more to be done. On this day everything rests.

In the Hebrew cosmology of the time, the souls of the just after death were thought to descend through the waters of the Great Abyss to a place of rest called Sheol, where they awaited their deliverance at the time of the Messiah. Accordingly, when Jesus died on Good Friday, his soul was believed by the first Christians to have passed through the waters of the Great Abyss to the place of Sheol, where he released the souls of the just. In Matthew's Gospel it is recorded that "After Jesus' resurrection they came forth from their tombs and entered the holy city and appeared to many."[14]

In the Old Testament, water is often the symbol of destruction. Water destroyed the wicked at the time of Noah. Water destroyed the Egyptians in the Red Sea when they tried to pursue the Israelites. At the same time, water also appears in the Old Testament as the symbol of life. In the Book of Genesis we read that the Spirit breathed over the waters of primeval chaos and they brought forth living creatures.

As Jesus' soul descended through the waters of the Great Abyss, the sins of the world which he was bearing were completely destroyed. In the ceremonies of baptism, we ritually descend into the waters of the Great Abyss together with Jesus, identifying with his holiness as he identified with our sinfulness. All our sins are destroyed in the waters of baptism. The one who emerges from the baptismal pool after being submerged in it joins Jesus in his ascent out of Sheol into the New Creation. The resurrection of Jesus is not the resuscitation of a corpse or the mere vindication of a just man. It is totally a new way of being. As Jesus' soul is reunited with his glorified body — baked, so to speak, in the limitless energy of the Spirit — he moves triumphantly into the heart of all creation. God's answer to Jesus' double-bind is to bestow upon him complete and unlimited participation in the Father's glory.

Creation is totally new in the light of the resurrection. The Sabbath belongs to the old world of sin that has passed away in the destruction of Christ's body on the cross. The New Creation, the eighth day, the day after the Sabbath, is the first day of eternal life in union with Christ, a day that will never end.

This new life is the significance of Jesus' death, his descent into Sheol and his resting in the tomb. The revelation of the enormous energy of the New Creation awaits the moment of his resurrection. God's first creative word, "Let there be light!"[15] becomes, "Let there be life!"

THE ANOINTING OF THE BODY OF JESUS

Afterward, Joseph of Arimathea asked Pilate's permission to remove the body of Jesus. Pilot granted it, so they came and took the body away. Nicodemus (the man who had first come to Jesus at night) likewise came bringing a mixture of myrrh and aloes which weighed about a hundred pounds. They took Jesus' body, and in accordance with Jewish burial custom, bound it up in wrappings of cloth with perfumed oils.

> In the place where he had been crucified there was a garden, and in the garden a new tomb in which no one had ever been laid. Because it was the Jewish Preparation Day, they laid Jesus there, for the tomb was close at hand. [John 19:38-42][16]

The text describes Nicodemus and the holy women anointing Christ's body with a generous portion of myrrh, aloes and perfumed oils in accordance with the Jewish custom.

We have already become acquainted with the symbolism of perfumed oil through the story of Mary of Bethany and her anointing of Jesus six days before his death. Oil is one of the symbols that appears frequently in the Old Testament as well as in the Gospel of John. In the Old Testament, the sick were anointed with oil, and kings and prophets were anointed with chrism (perfumed oil). In the sacrament of baptism, the catechumen is anointed with oil; in the sacrament of confirmation, the anointing is conferred with chrism (perfumed oil). The latter implies not only the bestowal of the Holy Spirit, symbolized by the anointing with oil, but the *perception* of the presence and action of the Spirit, symbolized by the delicious odor of the perfume.

When Mary of Bethany anointed Jesus with the perfume of great price — smashing the bottle and emptying the entire contents over him — she was affirming that he was no ordinary guest. She manifested her awareness that the Spirit had been imparted to Jesus not just in part, as was the case of the kings and prophets, but completely. She perceived that Jesus' sacred body was filled with the most costly perfume that ever existed, the Holy Spirit. Like the alabaster jar that she broke and emptied over his head, his body, too, was about to be broken and its sacred contents were to be poured out over the whole human family for its salvation.

Thus the outpouring of the Spirit as the fruit of Christ's sacrifice on the cross is magnificently expressed by Mary's lavish gesture. The text states that Jesus' body was anointed with a hundred pounds of myrrh, aloes and perfumed oils. Jesus' prophetic praise of Mary's action was thus thoroughly fulfilled: "What she has done is in anticipation of my burial."

In Christ, matter itself has become divine. At the moment of Christ's rising from the dead, the Holy Spirit rushed upon his body, anointing it with the fire of divine love, penetrating his sacred flesh until it was totally transformed not only into pure spirit, but into the divine nature itself. The entire material creation is now Christ's body. When we celebrate the

Eucharist, we are celebrating the glorification of the entire cosmos, present in some mysterious manner in the glorification of Christ's body. It is only a question of time until the fullness of that revelation becomes manifest.

In the Paschal Vigil, the liturgy makes extensive use of fire, which is a source of light, heat, and energy. The New Fire, symbolizing the Holy Spirit poured out over the world in the outpouring of Christ's blood, is blessed at the beginning of the Paschal Vigil. From that fire, the Paschal Candle, symbol of Christ's body waiting to be raised from the dead, is lit. When the celebrant touches the flame taken from the New Fire to the Paschal Candle, symbol of the glorified Christ, the eternal event of Jesus' resurrection becomes our own inner experience.

The assembly gathered for the Vigil walks in the darkness as the Paschal Candle leads the way to the sanctuary. This procession reenacts the deliverance of God's people from its oppressors in the Red Sea. Moses was sent to save his people from the bondage of Egypt. God said to him, "I have witnessed the affliction of my people in Egypt and have heard their cry . . . therefore I have come down to rescue them."[17]

In his passion Jesus equivalently says to us, "I have seen the affliction of the human family, and I have come down to free you for the full reception of the Spirit and the complete transformation of their nature into the divine — body, soul, and spirit."

In that sacred procession, reliving by faith the passage of the Israelites through the Red Sea and identifying with Christ's descent into Sheol through the waters of the Great Abyss, all our sins are once again utterly destroyed. As we enter the church, we receive a parted tongue of flame from the Paschal Candle, symbolizing a share of the Spirit. As we listen to the *Exultet*, the ancient hymn of thanksgiving chanted by a representative of the community, the candle we hold in our hands represents the light of faith in Christ's resurrection rising as an invincible conviction in our hearts. It is at that moment that the *Alleluia* is intoned.

The *Alleluia* is the song of ecstatic love, joy, praise, adoration and gratitude all rolled into one. It proclaims the triumph of God over death in every form. It is our response to the resolution of Christ's double-bind. As he passes into his glorification, he incorporates us into his own glorified body and shares with us his own happiness, the joy of eternal life. The *Alleluia* is the song of resurrection. It is the cry of those in whom the inner resurrection is taking place. Faith and confidence in Christ explode into the experience of divine union.

THE WOMEN VISIT THE TOMB

> When the Sabbath was over, Mary Magdalene, Mary the Mother of James, and Salome brought perfumed oils with which they intended to anoint the body of Jesus. Very early, just after sunrise, on the first day of the week they came to the tomb. They were saying to one another, "Who will roll back the stone from the entrance to the tomb for us?" When they looked, they found that the stone had been rolled back. (It was a huge one.) On entering the tomb, they saw a young man sitting at the right, dressed in a white robe. This frightened them thoroughly, but he reassured them: "You need not be amazed. You are looking for Jesus of Nazareth, the one who was crucified. He has been raised up; he is not here. See the place where they laid him. Go and tell his disciples and Peter, 'He is going ahead of you to Galilee where you will see him, just as he told you.' "
>
> They made their way out and fled from the tomb, bewildered and trembling; and because of their great fear, they said nothing to anyone. [Mark 16:1-8][18]

In his last moments on the cross Jesus was called upon by the Father to identify himself with the human family in all the consequences of sin. In doing so, Jesus experienced to the utmost degree the sense of alienation from God that is the result of coming to full reflective self-consciousness without the experience of divine union. This process happens to every human being; in the Christian tradition, it is called original sin.

The alienation that Jesus experienced in his passion caused him to die without the experience of the personal union with the Father that he had enjoyed throughout his earthly life. His holy soul, bearing our sins, descended into the destructive waters of the Great Abyss in order that our sinfulness might be utterly destroyed. Because of Christ's divine power, at the moment that sin was destroyed in the waters of the Great Abyss, these same waters instantly became the waters of eternal life. Christ gave to water the capacity to flow forever in superabundant mercy and to bring forth creatures capable of sharing his divine light, life and love.

As Christ's soul emerged from the waters made life-giving by the touch of his sacred humanity and re-entered his body, the sacrifice he had offered released within the bosom of the Father an incredible outpouring of divine light, life and love. The fire of the Holy Spirit, bursting with the fullness of divine energy, rushed upon his sacred remains. The perfumed oil of immense weight and value, symbolizing the Spirit, suggests the immense power that the Spirit exerted when the soul of Christ re-entered his body. In this reunion, the Father poured into the risen Jesus the whole of the divine essence — the utter riches, glory, and prerogatives of the divine nature — in a way that is utterly inconceivable to us.

In the Book of Revelation John tells of his vision of Christ as Lord of the universe: "His feet gleamed like polished brass refined in a furnace."[19] These words suggest that the Spirit glorified the flesh of Jesus until it was melted, so to speak, into divinity. It is this glorified flesh, united to the Eternal Word of God, that has entered into the heart of all creation and become one with all reality.

The reunion of the body and soul of Jesus took place in the secret of the night just before dawn, a moment that no one saw or witnessed. This is the event that is celebrated during the Paschal Vigil. The first rite of that sacred ceremony, as we saw, is the blessing of the New Fire, the symbol of the Spirit descending upon the precious blood of Christ poured out upon the ground. A spark is taken from the New Fire to light the Paschal Candle, celebrating the moment that Christ rose from the dead in glory. The Paschal Candle is the symbol of the pillar of fire by which God led the Israelites out of the slavery of Egypt into the Promised Land. The same presence and action is now leading us from sin and disbelief to higher levels of faith and consciousness. The passage of the Israelites through the Red Sea is re-enacted by the assembly as they walk through the darkened cloister or church into the sanctuary. The Paschal Candle symbolizes the risen Christ leading his people to the promised land of divine transformation. As the single flame atop the Paschal Candle is shared and becomes the possession of each member of the assembly, the whole church is gradually illumined without the original flame being diminished. Divine charity, the ripe fruit of Christ's resurrection, never diminishes; it is increased by being shared. Because of the intrinsic power of the Easter mystery, the Paschal Vigil is not a mere commemoration of Christ's resurrection; it awakens the experience of Christ rising in our inmost being and spreading the fire of his love throughout all our faculties.

At this point in the celebration of the Paschal Vigil, the great hymn of Easter is sung by the deacon. In this magnificent hymn in honor of the resurrection, we can feel welling up inside of us the enthusiasm of the Christian people of all time.

Rejoice, heavenly powers! Sing, choirs of angels!
Exult, all creation around God's throne!
Jesus Christ, our King, is risen!
Sound the trumpet of salvation!

Rejoice, O earth, in shining splendor,
radiant in the brightness of your King!
Christ has conquered! Glory fills you!
Darkness vanishes forever!...

This is our passover feast, when Christ,
the true Lamb, is slain...

This is the night when first you saved our fathers:
You freed the people of Israel from their slavery
and led them dry-shod through the sea.

This is the night when Christians everywhere,
washed clean of sin, and freed from all defilement,
are restored to grace and grow together in holiness.

This is the night when Jesus Christ broke the chains
of death and rose triumphant from the grave.
What good, indeed, would life have been to us,
had Christ not come as our Redeemer?

Father, how wonderful your care for us! How boundless
your merciful love! To ransom a slave, you gave away
your Son!

O happy fault! O necessary sin of Adam which gained
for us so great a Redeemer!...

The power of this night dispels all evil, washes guilt
away, and restores lost innocence...

O night truly blessed, when heaven is wedded to earth,
and man is reconciled with God!

After the chanting of the *Exultet*, everyone is seated and the lessons containing the biblical symbols highlighted by the hymn are explained. Then the *Alleluia* is sung and the saving presence and power of Christ is applied concretely to the community in the baptism of its catechumens.

Notice in the hymn there is the statement that this sacred night "restores lost innocence". This phrase, of course, refers to the Garden of Eden and the story of Adam and Eve. It recalls their loss of intimacy with God. The heart of the Easter mystery is our personal discovery of intimacy with God which scripture calls "innocence." It is the innocence arising from easy and continual exchange of the most delightful kind with God. This relationship casts out all fear.

In order to understand the meaning of scriptural innocence, we must distinguish it from the innocence of ignorance. The innocence of ignorance is the mindlessness that the animal world enjoys, the inability to reflect on oneself or to take responsibility for one's actions. The loss of that kind of innocence does not need to be regretted. Rather, rational consciousness is the greatest achievement of the evolutionary process to date.

At the same time, there is a sense in which we have known God before. This sense comes from the ontological unconscious, which is God remembering himself in us, so to speak. We have a deep-seated intuition that some indispensable relationship essential for our wellbeing and happiness is missing. The spiritual journey is a way of remembering our Source, what Meister Eckhart calls the "ground unconscious." The ground unconscious becoming conscious is our awakening to the Mystery of God's presence within us. This is the innocence to which scripture and the *Exultet* refer.

Easter is the awakening of divine life in us. "Christ is risen!" is not merely the cry of historical witnesses. It is the cry of all the people of God throughout the centuries who have realized Christ rising in them, not only in the form of emotional enthusiasm, but in the form of unshakable conviction. The light of Christ reveals the fact of our abiding union with him and its potential to transform every aspect of our lives.

MARY MAGDALENE MEETS THE RISEN CHRIST

Mary Magdalene was lingering outside the tomb, weeping. As she was giving vent to her tears she stooped to look into the tomb, and she saw two angels in white seated where the body had lain, one at the head, the other at the feet. "Woman," they said to her, "why are you weeping?"

"Because," she replied, "they have taken away my master and I do not know where they laid him." With this she turned around to look behind and saw Jesus standing by, but did not know that it was Jesus.

"Woman," Jesus said to her, "why are you weeping? Who is it you are looking for?" Taking him to be the gardener, she replied, "Sir, if you carried him away, tell me where you laid him. I want to remove him."

Then Jesus said, "Mary!" Turning around she said to him in Hebrew, "Raboni!" (which means "Master").

"Stop clinging to me," Jesus said to her. "I am ascending to the Father. Go therefore to my brothers and say to them, 'I am ascending to my Father and to your Father, to my God and to your God.'" Mary Magdalene went to carry the message to the disciples. [John 20:11-18][20]

The resurrection of Jesus is the first day of the New Creation. The events following the resurrection and the various appearances of Jesus to his disciples and friends are used in the liturgy to help us understand the significance of this central Mystery of our faith.

We have seen how Jesus died in the unresolved double-bind between identification with the human condition and the loss of personal union with the Father that is the inevitable result of this identification. The resurrection of Jesus is the resolution of that double-bind. It is the answer of the Father to the sacrifice of Jesus. It opened for us, as well as for him, a totally new life. It is the decisive moment in human history: as a result, divine union is now accessible to every human being.

The first resurrection scene is cast in a cosmic context. From the scriptural point of view, the garden in which the tomb of Jesus was situated reminds us of the garden of Eden. The two gardens are juxtaposed: in the first, the human family, in the persons of Adam and Eve, lost God's intimacy and friendship; in the second, Mary Magdalene (out of whom Jesus had cast seven devils) appears as the first recipient of the good news that intimacy and union with God are once again available.

She came to the tomb in great distress. The huge stone, symbol of the heavy weight of sin and the downward pull of the lower levels of consciousness, had been rolled away. When the women looked in, there was nothing in the tomb but the winding cloths with which Jesus had been buried. This caused Mary to think that his body had been stolen. In her great love for Jesus, she lingered outside the tomb after the other women had gone. She looked into the tomb again just to make sure, and now she saw two angels in white. They were surprised to see someone in tears on such a joyful occasion and said, "Woman, why are you weeping?"

She does not seem to have noticed that angels were speaking to her. She was totally absorbed in one thing only, and that was missing. She said to them, "If you have removed his body, tell me where you have put it and I will come and take it away." She was completely oblivious to the fact that Jesus' body would be too heavy for her to move. It had been anointed with a hundred pounds of myrrh, aloes and perfumed oil, so it was a hundred pounds heavier than before. But these considerations were obliterated by the intensity of her grief. Paying no further attention to these unusual personages, she started looking around in the garden. There she saw a man whom she presumed to be the gardener.

She was not mistaken. Jesus *is* the gardener in the garden of the New Creation. Because of her emotional turmoil, however, she does not recognize him. This is characteristic of the post-resurrection apparitions. It is only gradually that Jesus usually manifests himself. We can presume from this fact that he had acquired a new form. Apparently Jesus did not enter into his full glory right away; it was withheld so that he could spend time with his disciples. It is only at his ascension that he enters fully into the glory that the fire of the Holy Spirit initiated at the moment of his resurrection.

The "gardener" says with a certain irony, "Woman, whom are you looking for? Why are you weeping?" This question seems to have crystallized Mary's immense grief, and she poured out her heart in a jumble of words: "Tell me where you have laid him, sir, and I will remove him."

Jesus then spoke her name, "Mary!" Only he could say her name in that way. Instantly, with the whole of her being, she recognized him and in that moment *knew* that he had risen from the dead.

In the scripture, to be called by name has special significance. To call someone or something by name is to identify who or what it is. Adam, in paradise, named each beast and flower according to its essence. God often changed the names of prophets to fit their roles. By calling her by name, Jesus manifests his knowledge of everything in her life and his total acceptance of all that she is. This is the moment in which Mary realizes that Jesus loved her. This is the first step in her transformation.

In the Christian scheme of things, the movement from the human condition to divine transformation requires the mediation of a personal relationship with God. The personal love of Jesus facilitates the growth of this relationship. The experience of being loved by him draws the Christian out of all selfishness into deeper levels of self-surrender. How could this movement occur without the conviction of being personally loved by him? The simple utterance of one word, "Mary!" brought to focus all her longings.

Her response was to throw herself into the arms of Jesus as she cried out in her joy, "Master!"

The realization of being loved by God characterizes the first stage of contemplative prayer. It enables us to see God in all things. Mary's acceptance of that grace leads to a further insight; she becomes aware that she loves Jesus in return. Accordingly, she throws herself into his arms and clings to him. We are not told how long this embrace lasted, but through that experience she was raised to the next level of contemplative prayer, which is the capacity to see all things in God.

In this conversation, Jesus is raising Mary step-by-step through the progressive stages of contemplative prayer to divine union. Finally, he says to her, "Stop clinging to me! I have not yet risen to my Father. But, go and tell my brothers that I ascend to my Father and to your Father."

Those words are the manifesto of the New Creation! God is now not only the Father of Jesus Christ, not just the "Abba" whom Jesus has revealed out of his own personal experience of divine union. The Abba has now been given to us! The experience that Christ has of the Father is completely ours! Thus, the same relationship with the Father that Christ enjoys is rising up in Mary Magdalene — and in each of us as we assimilate the grace of Easter.

With these words of Jesus, Mary is sent to be the apostle of the apostles. What makes an apostle is divine love, nothing else. Since she now had within herself the experience of intimacy with the Father, bestowed upon her by Jesus, she is the one who proclaims to the apostles the message of Easter. "You, my brothers," Jesus says through her, "have been initiated into the reign of God, into my experience of the Father as Abba, the God of infinite compassion."

Jesus, in the plan of God, has opened the way to the highest states of consciousness. The pain and agony of self-consciousness, with its guilt-ridden sense of responsibility, has been replaced by the invitation to enter into the human potential for unlimited growth. The Garden of Eden is both a memory of what could be and a preview of what is to come. In the Garden of the Resurrection the full revelation of the Mystery of Christ is unveiled. And with that knowledge and experience, Mary reaches the third level of contemplative prayer, the abiding *state* of divine union, which is to see God giving himself in everything. This is the transformed consciousness of inner resurrection. And this is the Good News she was sent to announce to the apostles.

Adam and Eve were thrown out of the first garden as a result of the emergence of their self-consciousness apart from divine union. Mary was so rooted in the experience of divine union that the Garden of Paradise was inside her and she could never leave it. The Garden of Eden stands for a state of consciousness, not a geographical location. She is sent out of the garden, but with the abiding interior state the garden represents: the certitude of being loved by God, of loving him in return, and of God giving himself in every event and at every moment, both within or without. In this state, outside and inside are in harmony; they have become one. In the course of this conversation, the Ultimate Mystery becomes for Mary the Ultimate Presence, and the Ultimate Presence becomes the Ultimate Reality.

The outpouring of grace that we see in this first appearance of Jesus after his resurrection is God's response to Christ's sacrifice; it is his glorification in response to his utter humiliation. Like Mary Magdalene, Christ is also calling us by name as we celebrate the feast of his resurrection.

ON THE ROAD TO EMMAUS

Two disciples of Jesus that same day (the first day of the Sabbath) were making their way to a village named Emmaus, seven miles distant from Jerusalem, discussing as they went all that had happened. In the course of their lively exchange, Jesus approached and began to walk along with them. However, they were restrained from recognizing him. He said to them, "What are you discussing as you go your way?"

They halted in distress, and one of them, Cleopas by name, asked him, "Are you the only resident of Jerusalem who does not know the things that went on there these past few days?"

He said to them, "What things?"

They said, "All those that had to do with Jesus of Nazareth, a prophet powerful in word and deed in the eyes of God and all the people; however, our chief priests and leaders delivered him up to be condemned to death, and crucified him. We were hoping that he was the one who would set Israel free. Besides all this, today, the third day since all these things happened, some women of our group just brought us some astounding news. They were there at the tomb before dawn and failed to find his body, but returned with the tale that they had seen a vision of angels who declared he was alive. Some of our number went to the tomb and found it just as the women had said; but him they did not see."

Then he said to them, "What little sense you have! How slow you are to believe all that the prophets have announced! Did not the Messiah have to undergo all this so as to enter into his glory?" Beginning, then, with Moses and all the prophets, he interpreted for them every passage of scripture which referred to him.

By now they were near the village to which they were going, and he acted as if he were going farther. But they pressed him: "Stay with us. It is nearly evening — the day is practically over." So he went in and stayed with them.

When he had seated himself with them to eat, he took bread, pronounced the blessing, and then broke the bread and distributed it to them. With that their eyes were opened and they recognized him; whereupon he vanished from their sight. They said to one another, "Were not our hearts burning inside us as he talked to us on the road and explained the scriptures to us?"

They got up immediately and returned to Jerusalem, where they found the Eleven and the rest of the company assembled. They were greeted with, "The Lord has been raised! It is true! He has appeared to Simon." Then they recounted what had happened on the road and how they had come to know him in the breaking of the bread. [Luke 24:13-35][21]

This story shows us two of Jesus' disciples who represent the basic state of mind in which most of the disciples found themselves on the day of the resurrection. They were utterly discouraged. No one's career and message had ever been so thoroughly defeated and discredited in the public eye as had that of Jesus. Even his disciples and closest friends had left him and fled; indeed, he had been betrayed into the hands of the ecclesiastical and civil officials by one of his closest friends. The hopes of his disciples were in shreds.

It is clear from this text that the hopes of these two disciples were not in accord with the message that Jesus had been trying to communicate during his lifetime. One of the things they said when he asked for an explanation of their sadness was, "We were hoping that he was the one who would set Israel free." In other words, these disciples — and this may have been Judas' problem as well — had preconceived ideas about who the Messiah was to be and what he was to do. One of their expectations was that he would deliver Israel from the domination of the Roman Empire. In other words, they wanted a Messiah who would fit into the nationalistic aspirations of the Jewish people of that time. Although Jesus had made it clear that he would have nothing to do with political programs, he could not get this idea out of the heads of his disciples. Consequently, when he predicted well in advance that he would be delivered into the hands of the Gentiles and put to death, they did not hear what he said.

Our emotional programming is such that we rarely hear what we do not wish to hear. The disciples envisaged the reign of God as a political triumph, not as the mystery of God's intervention in their personal lives.

The two disciples had heard reports about women going to the tomb and not finding the body of Jesus. It does not seem to have occurred to them that if the women's report about the empty tomb were true, their report that Jesus had risen from the dead might also be true. The confused and disgruntled disciples were paralyzed by disappointment and grief.

Hiding his identity, Jesus appeared as a stranger, a fellow-traveler along the road, and asked, "Friends, what are you talking about, and why do you look so sad?" His friendly and courteous manner opened them up to dialogue, and they poured out the reasons for their distress.

Notice that the disciples were heading away from Jerusalem. They had evidently decided, despite what the women were reported to have said, that their part in the community of Jesus' disciples was over.

Jesus' response to their sad tale was, "How little sense you have! How slow you are to believe all that the prophets have announced!" Then, opening the scriptures to them, he began to put into perspective the true meaning of the Messiah. As they approached the outskirts of Emmaus, Jesus indicated that he was going further; he probably would have gone on unless they had urged him to stay with them.

He went in to the inn with them and sat down at table. It was now evening, the time of the evening sacrifice and the time that the Last Supper had been eaten. He took bread, pronounced the blessing and broke the bread. Then he distributed it to them just as they had seen him do many times before at common meals.

Later the disciples acknowledged to each other that their hearts were burning as Jesus explained the scriptures to them. This "burning" brought them to a high level of concentration and attentiveness. Suddenly, as Jesus broke the bread, the data of their external senses and their interior alertness connected. The intuition of faith saw through the outward appearance of

the stranger to the Reality. In front of them was the risen Christ! As soon
as they recognized him, he vanished from their eyes.

"They immediately turned around and went back to Jerusalem." There
they learned that Jesus had also appeared to Peter. During the course of
the day, the apostles had come to accept the fact of the resurrection, either
because they had been to the empty tomb or because Peter had seen the
Lord. More importantly, they were beginning to experience interiorly the
grace of the resurrection. The risen Christ was awakening within them,
enabling them to see the events of the past few days with the x-ray eyes
of faith.

Like the disciples of Emmaus, we, too, have our own ideas of Jesus
Christ, his message and his church. We, too, are conditioned by our
upbringing, early education, culture and life experience. The disciples could
not recognize Jesus as long as their mindset about who he was and what
he was to do were in place. When Jesus demolished their blindness with
his explanation of the scriptures, their vision of him began to assume a more
realistic tone. The price of recognizing Jesus is always the same: our idea
of him, of the church, of the spiritual journey, of God himself has to be
shattered. To see with the eyes of faith we must be free of our culturally-
conditioned mindsets. When we let go of our private and limited vision,
he who has been hidden from us by our pre-packaged values and preconceived
ideas causes the scales to fall from our eyes. He was there all the time. Now
at last we perceive his Presence. With the transformed vision of faith, we
return to the humdrum routines and duties of daily life, but now, like Mary
Magdalene, we recognize God giving himself to us in everyone and in
everything.

THE APPEARANCE IN THE UPPER ROOM

Late in the evening of that same day, the first day of the
week, although the doors of the place where the disciples had
gathered were bolted for fear of the authorities, Jesus came and
stood before them."Peace be to you," he said. [John 20:19]

They were in a complete panic, fancying they were seeing
a ghost. "Why are you disturbed?" he said to them, "and why
do you let doubts come into your minds? Look at my hands
and my feet. Surely it is my very self! Feel me, and convince

yourselves; no ghost has flesh and bones such as you see I have!"
With that, he showed them his hands and his feet.

But they still refused to believe; it was too good to be true,
and continued in their perplexity. So he said to them, "Have
you something here to eat?" Then they offered him a piece of
broiled fish which he accepted and ate before their eyes.

He said to them, "These events are the fulfillment of what
I predicted to you when I was still with you, namely that
anything ever written concerning me — in the Law of Moses,
in the prophets, or in the psalms — must be fulfilled." He then
gave them the key to the understanding of the scriptures. "This,"
he said to them, "is the gist of the scripture: The messiah must
suffer, and on the third day rise from the dead. Furthermore:
In his name the need of a change of heart and the forgiveness
of sins must be preached to all the nations." [Luke 24:37-47][22]

This appearance of Jesus took place after the two disciples had returned
to Jerusalem and heard the other disciples joyfully announce, "It is true!
The Lord is risen! He has appeared to Simon!"

In the midst of their conversation, Jesus suddenly appeared, throwing
the group into a state of panic. They thought he was a ghost, even though
they had just been talking about his appearance to Peter. Jesus' words to
them are fraught with significance: "Peace be to you!" Peace is the tranquility
of order. It is true security. True security is the direct consequence of divine
union. There is nothing wrong with desiring security. Everybody wants
it and needs it. The problem is that we look for it in the wrong places.
Peace is the result of the principal benefit of Christ's resurrection — the
experience of the divine Presence as permanent. Peace is the treasure that
Jesus triumphantly and joyfully bestows, or tries to bestow, on his crushed
and demoralized apostles.

"Peace be with you!" he said again. But these words made no impression
on them because they were preoccupied with the fear that they might be
seized and put in jail as his disciples. They were a little band of frightened
people just beginning to revive from their crushing bereavement. Suddenly,
Jesus is visibly in their midst. Their first thought probably was, "I thought
we bolted the door!"

Jesus had now passed beyond spatial limitations. He came in through
the bolted door. Or maybe he was already present on another level of reality,
invisible to the disciples. He had previously said to them, "Wherever two

or three are gathered in my name, I am there with you." In any case, to the disciples' great astonishment he was there in their midst, and their first reaction was, "It's a ghost!"

He said to them, "Why are you disturbed?" As usual, Jesus goes to the heart of their motivation. At this point, their emotional programs and their imaginations were working overtime: they were projecting a ghost where there was obviously a person of flesh and blood. They did not even have the courtesy to invite him to sit down.

Jesus, perhaps with a certain amusement, asked them again, "Why do you let doubts arise in your minds?" He was trying to reassure them.

Failing in that approach, he tried to calm them by engaging their external senses. "Look at my hands and my feet. Isn't it I?" Holding out his hands to them to satisfy their curiosity, he said, "Feel me and convince yourselves." "No ghost has flesh and bones such as I have!"

Yet still they could not accept the plain fact of his visible presence among them. It was too good to be true! As they lingered in their perplexity, he continued to try to put them at ease.

"Have you something to eat?" he asked. Nothing could convince us more quickly that an apparent ghost is a real human being than a request for something to eat. The disciples frantically looked around and came up with a piece of broiled fish.

This detail is not without significance. Everything in the Gospel narratives of the resurrection has symbolic overtones. Fish, at the time these Gospels were written, had already become the symbol of Christ or one of his followers. In Greek the first two letters for *Christ* are also the first two letters for the word "fish". If a fish is the symbol of Christ, a broiled fish is the symbol of his transformed humanity. Jesus is standing before them, but in a transfigured humanity.

After he had consumed the broiled fish, the disciples began to calm down. At last they were ready to receive his instructions. "These events," he said, "are the fulfillment of what I told you would happen." He had predicted on numerous occasions that he would be handed over to the authorities, put to death and rise on the third day, but the disciples' emotional blocks had not allowed them to hear what he was saying.

"Everything written about me in the Law of Moses, in the prophets and in the psalms must be fulfilled," Jesus continued. Then he gave them the key to *understanding* the scriptures. The key to understanding the scriptures enables one to perceive the spiritual meaning contained in the text. Jesus showed the disciples that the meaning of certain prophetic texts was fulfilled in the events that had just taken place: "The Messiah must suffer and on the third day rise from the dead, and that in his name the need for a change of heart and the forgiveness of sins must be preached to all the nations."

The need for a change of heart is the need to change the direction in which we are looking for happiness. The same key that opens the scriptures opens the door to happiness.

The forgiveness of sins and the consequent restoration of friendship with God is the great triumph of Jesus' sacrifice. This is the true security that every human heart yearns for. Jesus' sacrifice frees us from the separate-self sense and from the alienation that flows from it. This is the peace which the world cannot give. The peace of Christ comes from the inner experience of his resurrection, the realization of the union of our true self with the Ultimate Reality.

CHRIST SATISFIES THOMAS' DOUBTS

Late in the evening of that day, the first day of the week, although the doors of the place where the disciples were gathered were bolted for fear of the authorities, Jesus came and stood before them and said, "Peace be with you!" With that, he let them see his hands and his side. The disciples were delighted to see the Lord.

Then Jesus said to them again, "Peace be with you! As the Father has sent me, so also I am sending you." With this, he breathed on them and said: "Receive the Holy Spirit. Whenever you remit anyone's sins, they are remitted; when you retain anyone's sins, they are retained."

Thomas, one of the twelve, was not with the group when Jesus came, so the other disciples said to him, "We have seen the Master!" But he replied, "Unless I see in his hands the print of the nails, and put my finger into the place where the nails were, and lay my hand into his side, I am not going to believe!"

Eight days later, his disciples were again in the room and Thomas was with them. Jesus came, though the doors were bolted, and standing before them said, "Peace be to you!" He then addressed Thomas: "Let me have your finger; put it here, and look at my hands. Now let me have your hand, and lay it into my side. And do not be incredulous, but believe."

Then Thomas burst out into the words, "My Master and my God!"

Because you have seen me," Jesus said to him, "is that why you believed? Blessed are those that have not seen and yet believe." [John 20:19-31][23]

The two great gifts of Jesus to his disciples on the day of his resurrection, the first day of the New Creation, were the forgiveness of sin and the restoration of divine union. But a still greater gift is implied: he gave them the Holy Spirit, the Source of the forgiveness of sin and of divine union.

The events of the resurrection place before us various aspects of the Paschal Mystery including the meaning of the New Creation. Let us take a look at the intriguing narrative of the apostle Thomas and his particular response to the news of the resurrection.

Thomas was not present when the disciples had their first meeting with the risen Christ. His story is regarding the caliber of the disciples whom Jesus chose. Here is an apostle who had spent three years in the intimate company of Jesus undergoing intensive spiritual training, listening daily to his teaching, and witnessing many of his miracles. Yet it is obvious from this event that Thomas was still heavily under the influence of his emotional programs for happiness. Because Jesus chose to visit the apostles at a time when Thomas was absent, his reaction was, "How come I was left out? What's wrong with me? How do these other guys rate?"

As Thomas thought about the situation, his indignation continued to increase. The other apostles kept telling him, "We have seen the Lord!" Deep down inside, his response was resentment rather than joy. He felt neglected, rejected, frustrated, and, finally, enraged.

What was Thomas thinking? "If Jesus is not going to include me, I'm not going to include him. If he doesn't want me, I don't want him either." It was the childish reaction of withdrawal. He would price himself out of the market, so to speak. Have there ever been more outrageous conditions that a little clay man demanded of the Almighty in exchange for his faith? "Unless I see in his hands the print of the nails, *and* unless I put my finger into the place where the nails were; *and* lay my hand into his side, I am not going to believe!"

This was the equivalent of saying, "Goodbye! I am through with you guys. I am through with Jesus."

We do not know how long Thomas nursed his bitterness, hurt feelings and sense of rejection. It did not make matters any better to observe the other apostles ecstatic with joy. Somehow they persuaded him to join them a week later for supper. We are not told why Thomas condescended to join them but we read: "Eight days later his disciples were once again in the room and Thomas with them. Jesus came, though the doors were bolted, and standing before them said, 'Peace be with you.' "

Jesus looked around the room until his eyes rested on Thomas. Thomas, at this point, was looking for a hole in the floor into which he could crawl. "My God! What have I said?" The outrageous conditions he had laid down in exchange for his faith struck home in their full clarity. Jesus looked straight at him. Maybe Jesus was smiling. Thomas foresaw what was going to happen.

Jesus said, "Thomas, let me have your finger. Put it here in my hands! And now let me have your hand. Place it here in my side!" Notice the detail with which Jesus meets his outrageous demands: point-by-point and word-for-word. "And do not be incredulous but believe!"

That final remark pierced Thomas to the heart. He recognized the incredible goodness of Jesus in submitting himself to his demands. This loving acquiescence to every detail of his ridiculous demands placed Thomas in a state of complete vulnerability. Like Adam and Eve, he was being called out of the woods, out of the underbrush where his false self had been hiding from the truth, into the stark reality of Jesus' love. What could he say? His response was the total gift of himself: "My Master and my God!"

We do not know whether Thomas actually put his hand into Jesus' side. But we do know that he had all the evidence he needed. He put his faith in the risen Jesus, perhaps to a greater degree than the other disciples. One marvelous effect of divine mercy is that the harder you fall, the higher you rise, provided you accept the humiliation. "When I am weak," Paul confessed, "then I am strong."[24]

Jesus added one final remark: "Blest are those who have not seen and yet believe!" As if to say, "I am happy, Thomas, that you have found faith. But leaving you out of my first visit was not a rejection but an invitation to a greater grace." It was an invitation to put your faith in me on the basis of your own inner experience."

The resurrection of Jesus is not only an historical event. The words of Jesus to Thomas suggest something more. They might be paraphrased as follows: "You based your faith on seeing me, Thomas, but there is greater happiness — to believe in my resurrection because you experience its effects within yourself."

This, of course, is an important message for us. It tells us that it is far better to relate to the risen Christ on the basis of pure faith that rests not on appearances, feelings, external evidence, or what other people say, but on our personal experience of the Christ-life rising up and manifesting its fruits within us. This is the living faith that empowers us to act under the influence of the Spirit — the same Spirit that Jesus breathed upon the apostles on the evening of his resurrection.

CHRIST APPEARS TO HIS FRIENDS AT THE SEA OF GALILEE

On a later occasion Jesus showed himself again to the disciples, this time by the Lake of Tiberias. He did so under the following circumstances: Simon Peter, Thomas, Nathaniel, the sons of Zebedee, and two other of his disciples happened to be together. Peter said to them, "I am going fishing." "We will go with you," they replied.

So they set out and got into the boat and during the entire night they caught nothing. But just as day was breaking Jesus stood on the beach. The disciples did not know, however, that it was Jesus. "Well, lads," Jesus said, "have you any fish?"

"No," they replied.

"Cast your net to the right of the boat," he said to them, "and you will find something." They cast it and now they were not strong enough to haul it up into the boat because of the great number of fish in it.

Then the disciple whom Jesus loved said to Peter, "It is the Master!" As soon as Peter learned that it was the Master, he girt his upper garment about him and plunged into the lake. Meanwhile, the other disciples came in the boat — for they were not far from the shore, only about two-hundred yards — dragging along the net full of fish.

When they had come ashore, they noticed hot embers on the ground, with fish lying on the fire, and bread. Jesus said to them, "Bring some of the fish you caught just now." So Peter boarded the boat and hauled the net up on the beach. It was full of fish, 153 in all, and in spite of the great number the net did not break. "Come now," Jesus said to them, "and have breakfast." Not one of his disciples could find it in his heart to ask him, "Who are you?" They knew it was the Master.

Then Jesus approached, took bread in his hands, and gave them of it. He did the same with the fish.

This was now the third time Jesus showed himself to the disciples after he had risen from the dead. [John 21:1-14][25]

This text has an unmistakable nostalgia about it. One senses the leisurely pace of this third appearance of Jesus to the apostles.

Some of the apostles had gathered together in their old home town. He had said to them, "I go before you into Galilee. There you will see me." So they went back home according to his instructions and were hanging around their old haunts by the Lake of Tiberias, where they had earned their living before Jesus had called them out of their respective businesses to join him in proclaiming the reign of God.

Jesus had said he would meet them there. But where was he? Peter said to the other disciples, " How about going for a catch?" The other disciples said, "Fine, we'll go with you."

So they got into a boat and rowed out into the middle of the lake. They fished all day without a nibble. Twilight came; no bites. Night fell, and they were still sitting in the middle of the lake waiting for a catch. They tried their nets first on one side and then on the other. They rowed up and down the lake. It got darker and darker. The moon rose and set, and still they remained out on the lake. It was a night full of effort but no fish.

As they waited for the dawn, they grew more and more disgruntled. They were tired, cold and irritable. They had long since given up talking and sat slumped in the boat, glowering at the lake. They were now only a few hundred yards offshore. All at once, on the beach, emerging slowly from the shadows, was the outline of a man. As the light increased, the stranger became more and more visible. After a long time he called out to them in a friendly manner, "Lads, did you catch anything?"

They exchanged a few knowing glances. Couldn't this man figure out that a boatload of fishermen would not be sitting there at that hour if they had caught anything?

So they shouted back, "Naw!" The stranger, not put off by their unfriendly response, called back, "Try casting your net to the right side of the boat. Then you will catch something."

They said to each other, "Who is this guy, trying to tell us what to do?" We've been here all night. We know there are no fish in this lake." But one of them said, "We have nothing to lose."

So for the umpteenth time they grabbed the net, pulled it in and lowered it on the right side of the boat. All of a sudden there was an immense tug. A huge school of fish had swum into the net. In a moment the men were hanging onto the net for dear life and the boat was tipping dangerously to the side. It is the Lord!" John exclaimed. This is the second time the Gospel records a fishless night — a night full of effort and no result. It is a lively symbol of our experience interminable purification, giving way to the dawn of inner resurrection.

As soon as Peter heard that the stranger was Jesus, he jumped into the sea and swam ashore. The other disciples dragged the boat to shore and pulled the net onto the beach. There they noticed that Jesus had prepared a fire and a fish was broiling on top of it. Jesus, the breakfast cook, said to Peter, "Bring some of the fish that you have just caught."

While Peter went to look through the catch, the other apostles were in the process of counting them. It took awhile to count to a hundred and fifty-three fish, to select the best ones and to cook them. When everything was ready, Jesus said to them, "Come and have breakfast." Not one of the disciples could find it in his heart to ask, "Who are you?" They knew it was the Lord.

They all sat down. Jesus took the bread in his hands, said the blessing, broke it and gave it to them. He did the same with the fish. As they sat in silence consuming the meal, they recognized an unmistakable shift in their relationship with him. A meal together is a symbol of belonging. Before it had always meant conversation, laughter and singing. This was a new level of belonging. Their former relationship with Jesus was coming to an end and a new relationship was being communicated to them at a far deeper level. This sharing was not by word of mouth, nor by ideas or feelings, but by the Spirit dwelling in their inmost being, a far better form of communication than the one they had before. This is the relationship Jesus was referring to when he rebuked Thomas and pointed out to him that to believe on the basis of personal experience is a greater gift than to believe on the basis of external evidence.

The fifty days during which Jesus revealed himself to his disciples brought them out of their discouragement and into close relationship with the divine Spirit whom he had promised to send them. The disciples were brought from a merely human relationship with Jesus to the interior exchange that is proper to those who are advancing in faith and in sensitivity to the inspirations of the Spirit.

THE ASCENSION

> After speaking with them, the Lord Jesus was taken up into heaven and took his seat at God's right hand. The Eleven went forth and preached everywhere. [Mark 16:19-20]

By becoming a human being Christ annihilated the dichotomy between matter and spirit. In the Person of the Divine-human Being, a continuum between the divine and the human has been established. Thus, God's plan is not only to spiritualize the material universe, but to make matter itself divine. This he has already done in the glorified humanity of his Son. The grace bestowed on us by the Ascension of Jesus is the divinization of our humanity. Our individuality is permeated by the Spirit of God through the grace of the Ascension and more specifically through the grace of Pentecost. Thus we, in Christ, are also annihilating the dichotomy between matter and spirit. Our life is a mysterious interpenetration of material experience, spiritual reality and the divine Presence.

The key to being a Christian is to know Jesus Christ with the whole of our being. It is important to know his sacred humanity through our senses and to reflect upon it with our reason, to treasure his teaching and example in our imagination and memory, and to imitate him by a life of moral integrity. But this is only the beginning. It is to the transcendent potential in ourselves — to our mind which opens up to unlimited truth, and to our will which reaches out for unlimited love — that Christ addresses himself in the Gospel with particular urgency.

Not only is it important to know Jesus Christ with the whole of our being; it is also important to know Jesus Christ in the whole of *his* being. We must know Christ, first of all, in his sacred humanity and historical reality and, more precisely, in his passion, which was the culminating point of his life on earth. The essential note of his passion is the emptying of his divinity. We enter into his emptying by accepting the emptying process in our own life, by laying aside our false self and by living in the presence of God, the source of our being.

We must know Christ, however, not only in his human nature — his passion and emptying — but also in his divinity. This is the grace of the resurrection. It is the empowerment to live his risen life. It is the grace not to sin. It is the grace to express his risen life in the face of our inner poverty without at the same time ceasing to feel it.

The grace of the Ascension offers a still more incredible union, a more entrancing invitation to unbounded life and love. This is the invitation to enter into the cosmic Christ — into his divine person, the Word of God, who has always been present in the world. And he has always been present in a saving way because of God's foreknowledge of his incarnation, death, and resurrection. Christ is "the light that enlightens everyone" [John 1:9] — the God who is secretly at work in the most unexpected and hidden ways. This is the Christ who disappeared in his Ascension beyond the clouds, not into some geographical location, but into the heart of all creation. In particular, he has penetrated the very depths of our being, our separate-self sense has melted into his divine Person, and now we can act under the direct influence of his Spirit. Thus, even if we drink a cup of soup or walk down the street, it is Christ living and acting in us, transforming the world from within. This transformation appears in the guise of ordinary things — in the guise of our seemingly insignificant daily routine.

The Ascension is Christ's return to the heart of all creation where he dwells now in his glorified humanity. The mystery of his Presence is hidden throughout creation and in every part of it. At some moment of history, which prophecy calls the Last Day, our eyes will be opened and we will see reality as it is, which we know now only by faith. That faith reveals that Christ, dwelling at the center of all creation and of each individual member of it, is transforming it and bringing it back, in union with himself, into the bosom of the Father. Thus, the maximum glory of the Trinity is achieved through the maximum sharing of the divine life with every creature according to its capacity. This is "the mystery hidden for ages in God" [Eph. 3:9].

The grace of the Ascension is the triumphant faith that believes that God's will is being done no matter what happens. It believes that creation is already glorified, though in a hidden manner, as it awaits the full revelation of the children of God.

The grace of the Ascension enables us to perceive the irresistible power of the Spirit transforming everything into Christ despite any and all appearances to the contrary. In the misery of the ghetto, the battlefield, the concentration camp; in the family torn by dissension; in the loneliness of the orphanage, old-age home, or hospital ward — whatever we see that seems to be disintegrating into grosser forms of evil — the light of the Ascension is burning with irresistible power. This is one of the greatest intuitions of faith. This faith finds Christ not only in the beauty of nature, art, human friendship and the service of others, but also in the malice and injustice of people or institutions, and in the inexplicable suffering of the innocent. Even there it finds the same infinite love expressing the hunger of God for humanity, a hunger that he intends to satisfy.

Thus, in Colossians, Paul does not hesitate to cry out with his triumphant faith in the Ascension: "Christ is all and in all"[26] — meaning now, not just in the future. At this very moment we too have the grace to see Christ's light shining in our hearts, to feel his absorbing Presence within us, and to perceive in every created thing — even in the most disconcerting — the presence of his light, love and glory.

III

The Pentecost Mystery

If you love me and obey the commands I give you, I will ask the Father and he will give you another Paraclete — to be with you always: the spirit of truth, whom the world cannot accept because it neither sees him nor recognizes him; but you can recognize him because he remains with you and will be within you. [John 14:15-17]

INTRODUCTION

The period of preparation for the feast of Pentecost is brief (just ten days) because the two previous seasons have served as a remote preparation and have thoroughly prepared us for it.

Pentecost is, at the same time, the principal and crowning feast of the theological idea of divine love. It is, in fact, the crowning feast of the whole liturgical year. The rest of the year examines the teaching and example of Jesus in the light of Pentecost, that is, from the perspective of divine love.

THE FEAST OF PENTECOST

On the last and great day of the feast, Jesus stood and cried
out: "If any one is thirsty, let that person come to me and drink.
The one who believes in me, as Scripture said: 'From his
innermost being shall flow rivers of living water'". [John 7:37-39]

Each feast of the Liturgical Year is both an event to be celebrated and
a grace to be received. The grace of Christmas is to know Christ in his
humanity. The grace of Epiphany is to know him in his divinity. The grace
of Holy Week is to know him in his emptying and dying. The grace of
Easter is to know him in his triumph over sin and death. The grace of the
Ascension is to know him as the cosmic Christ. It is to know the glorified
Christ, who has passed, not into some geographical location, but into the
heart of all creation.

The cosmic Christ, revealed in the Mystery of the Ascension, manifests
our true self and the inner nature of all reality. What is manifested is the
living, vibrant Spirit, filling us and all things with boundless light, life and
love. The Spirit is always present, yet always coming. That is because the
Divine- actuality becomes present in a new way each time we move to a
new level of spiritual awareness. The Spirit has been given; yet he is always
waiting to be received so that he can give himself again, and more completely.
What then is the special grace of Pentecost?

On the day of his resurrection, Jesus breathed his Spirit upon his disciples,
saying: "Receive the Holy Spirit."[1] On the day of the Ascension, forty days
later, he "charged them not to depart from Jerusalem, but to wait for the
promise of the Father . . . before many days, you shall be baptized with the
Holy Spirit."[2]

The Spirit, then, is not given only once. He is an ongoing promise,
an endless promise — a promise that is always fulfilled and always being
fulfilled, because the Spirit is infinite and boundless and can never be fully
plumbed.

The Spirit is the ultimate promise of the Father. A promise is a free
gift. No one is bound to make a promise. Once a promise is made, however,
one is bound. When God binds himself, it is with absolute freedom, absolute
fidelity. The Spirit, as promise, is a gift, not a possession. He is a promise
that has been communicated; hence never to be taken back, since God is

infinitely faithful to his promises. Note that the communication is by way of gift, not possession. Like the air we breathe, we can have all that we wish to take into our lungs; but it does not belong to us. If we try to take possession of it — stuff it in a closet for safekeeping — our efforts will be in vain. Air is not made to be possessed, and neither is the Spirit.

The divine Spirit is all gift but will not acquiesce to a possessive attitude. He is all ours as long as we give him away. "The wind blows where it wills and you hear the sound of it, but you do not know when it comes or whither it goes; so it is with everyone who is born of the Spirit."[3] In these words, Jesus explained to Nicodemus and to us that we have no control over the Spirit. In fact, it is in giving him away that we manifest that we truly have received him. He is the supreme gift, but supremely himself, supremely free.

The Spirit of God, the promise of the Father, sums up in himself all the promises of Christ. For they all point to him. The Incarnation is a promise. The passion and death of Jesus are promises. His resurrection and Ascension are each a promise. Pentecost itself, the outpouring of the Spirit, is a promise. All are promises and pledges of the divine Spirit, present and to be received at every moment. He is the last, the greatest and the completion of all God's promises, the living summary of them all. Faith in him is faith in the whole of revelation. Openness and surrender to his guidance is the continuation of God's revelation in us and through us. It is to be involved in the redemption of the world and in the divinization of the cosmos. To know that Christ is all in all and to know his Spirit, the ongoing promise of the Father — this is the grace of Pentecost.

Between God and us, two extremes meet: He who is everything and we who are nothing at all. It is the Spirit who makes us one with God and in God, just as the Word is with God and is God — the Word by nature, we by participation and communication. Jesus prayed for this unity at the Last Supper. Many of his words on that occasion find their fulfillment and ultimate significance in the outpouring of the Spirit into our minds and hearts. Jesus said, "The glory you have given to me, I have given to them, that they may be one as we are one. I in them and you in me, that they may become perfectly one."[4]

The Spirit is the gift of God welling up in the Trinity from the common heart of the Father and the Son. He is the overflow of the divine life into the sacred humanity of Jesus, and then into the rest of us, his members.

"If anyone thirst, let him come to me and drink. He who believes in me, as the scripture has said, 'Out of his heart will flow rivers of living water.'"[5]

John tells us that Jesus was speaking of the Spirit when he uttered these words. The Spirit is the stream of living water which wells up in those who believe. It is the same Spirit that causes our hearts to rejoice because of the confidence that he inspires in God as Father. Abba, the word that spontaneously wells up in us, sums up our intimacy with God and our awareness of being not only with God as friend to friend, but in God. We are penetrated by God and penetrating into God, through the mysterious, all-enveloping, all-absorbing and all-embracing Spirit.

Jesus in his priestly prayer for his disciples prayed "that they may all be one; as you, Father, are in me, and I in you, that they also may be in us."[6] It is the Spirit who causes us to be one in the Body of Christ. We have all received the same Spirit, enlivening us and causing us to be in Christ, in the Father, in the Spirit.

We are in God and God is in us, and the unifying force is the Spirit. To live in the Spirit is the fulfillment of every law and commandment, the sum of every duty to each other, and the joy of oneness with everything that is.

IV

Ordinary Time

"I came that they may have life and have it to the full." [John 10:10]

INTRODUCTION

Ordinary Time is time from the perspective of Pentecost; time that has been transformed by the eternal values introduced by Jesus through his entrance into the space-time continuum of human experience. Every moment of chronological time is now the precious present in which eternal values are being offered, communicated and transmitted. Chronological and eternal time intersect in the mystery of the present moment and become one: the stream of time and eternity are co-terminus. The liturgy, under the influence of the Spirit, examines the teaching and example of Jesus from this contemplative perspective.

In this section examples from Jesus' teachings as expressed in the beatitudes and the parables along with several incidents of his ministry are presented to show how ordinary life is transformed by the power of the Gospel and by the divine light, life and love transmitted through the liturgy. In this sense, Ordinary Time is in fact totally extraordinary — time that has been transformed or time to be transformed.

THE BEATITUDES

The ripe fruit of the grace of Pentecost is the practice of the beatitudes. The beatitudes are acts of virtue inspired by the Spirit and which manifest the risen life of Christ within us.

TRUE HAPPINESS

When he saw the crowds, Jesus went up on the mountainside. After he had sat down his disciples gathered around him, and he began to teach them:
"How blest are the poor in spirit: the reign of God is theirs.
Blest too are the sorrowing; they shall be consoled.
Blest are the lowly; they shall inherit the land.
Blest are they who hunger and thirst for holiness; they shall have their fill.
Blest are they who show mercy; mercy shall be theirs.
Blest are the single-hearted for they shall see God.
Blest too are the peacemakers; they shall be called sons of God.
Blest are those persecuted for holiness' sake; the reign of God is theirs.
Blest are you when they insult you and persecute you and utter every kind of slander against you because of me.
Be glad and rejoice, for your reward is great in heaven; they persecuted the prophets before you in the very same way." [Matt. 5:1-12][1]

The beginning of the Sermon on the Mount contains a number of affirmations called the beatitudes that summarize Jesus' teaching about the nature of true happiness. Each begins with the term "blest," which means, "Oh, how happy you would be!" The first three beatitudes are aimed at demolishing the values of the first three energy centers and the programs for happiness on which they are based. Those who are motivated by one of these three energy centers have designed for themselves a program for human misery.

The first three energy centers are elaborate programs for happiness that evolved at a pre-rational age and that are now heavily defended. Hence, the emphasis in Jesus' ministry on repentance, which means "change the direction in which you are looking for happiness." The beatitudes came out of the heart of Jesus when he looked at the multitudes that were following him and realized with infinite compassion that "they were like sheep without a shepherd," all going their own way — that is, nowhere at a great rate. "Jetting to nowhere" summarizes in technological language the projects of the first three energy centers. The beatitudes give us some insight into how to dismantle them and to move toward true happiness.

The first three beatitudes might be summed up by the commandment, "Love your neighbor as yourself." If that commandment were lived out, it would quickly dismantle the false-self system. We cannot possibly love our neighbor as ourself so long as we are acting out fantastic demands for security and survival, affection and esteem, and power and control.

The next four beatitudes are aimed at higher states of consciousness. Once love of neighbor has been established, divine love begins to unfold its secrets. The last four beatitudes might be summed up by Jesus' commandment, "love one another as I have loved you." This dimension of love is more profound and all-inclusive than the commandment to love your neighbor as yourself.

Let us consider the first beatitude, "How blest are the poor in spirit: the reign of God is theirs." What is the reign of God? It is what God does in us. It certainly is not a rule of life of our own making. It is the openness that allows God to enter our lives at any time. Hence, it presupposes a flexibility to adjust to events and circumstances and a willingness to let go of our own plans in favor of the inspirations that come from the Spirit.

Who are the poor in spirit? The poor in spirit are the oppressed, the downtrodden and the despised in a particular culture. They are the nobodies, the insignificant, the people who don't rate. The term embraces those who are not necessarily materially poor, although that can be one of the factors that makes the destitute objects of contempt for those who are better off. Evangelical poverty addresses itself to those who suffer any form of human privation. The additional words "in spirit" point to the fact that to experience this beatitude, it is not enough to be materially poor or to suffer affliction, it is necessary to accept whatever the painful condition is. The poor in spirit are those who are willing to endure affliction of whatever kind for God's sake.

The final beatitude declares those who are persecuted for justice or truth's sake to be especially happy because they have a special claim to the reign of God and to the fullness of happiness. One is not normally persecuted for inaction, but for trying to change unjust societal structures. This warns us that the poor in spirit are not simply passive in the face of the oppressive circumstances in which they find themselves. Their first movement or response, it is true, is to accept what is. But God's will may also suggest that we act to correct, improve, or change unjust structures or oppressive situations in ways that are in accord with God's will and as the Holy Spirit may inspire.

To accept everything passively could indicate a passive-dependent personality that leans too heavily on pleasing others, especially authority figures, in order to bolster up one's fragile sense of security. Passive acceptance could also result from years of suffering some form of physical, psychological, social, economic or religious oppression which has finally exhausted one's capacity to resist injustice anymore or to take any significant initiative to oppose it. Oppression of whatever kind, if it continues for a long period of time, crushes the potential of the will to act and relegates its victims to the enormous dump of human inertia and indifference.

The poor in spirit, then, are those who accept affliction actively, not passively. They willingly accept the situation for what it is — a fact of life — and then work to make it better. This is co-creating the world with God, and this is the basic vocation of human beings. It is the message of the Garden of Eden.[2]

Of all the people who have lived on earth, Jesus, the Son of God, was the most free to choose where to be born, where to live and where to die. His choices are striking, to say the least. They bear no resemblance to the programs of the first three energy centers that everyone else is plagued with.

First of all, he lived in a town that was regarded as totally insignificant. One text reads, "Can any good come out of Nazareth?"[3] Or again, Jesus insisted on being baptized by John the Baptist. When John objected, Jesus replied, "We must do this if we would fulfill all of God's demands."[4] The baptism of John was a call to repentance. Jesus wanted to reinforce that call by experiencing John's baptism himself. Baptism is a commitment to free oneself from excessive demands for security and survival, affection and esteem, and power and control. The beatitude of the poor in spirit focuses on the security center that constantly demands more and better of everything in order to feel secure.

Jesus could have been an austere ascetic like John the Baptist, but instead he chose a middle way. He ate with sinners and drank wine, two things that the disciples of John would not think of doing. He talked to women in public, something that a rabbi at that time was not supposed to do. Jesus was free from the conformity level of morality that his contemporaries were locked into. He would not conform to local custom merely for the sake of satisfying the religious sensibilities of the time.

In the end, Jesus died between two criminals, betrayed by a friend and abandoned by his disciples. No public benefactor was ever so thoroughly disgraced from every point of view and rejected by both the religious and civil authorities. In the example of Jesus' life, being is more important than doing; it is not how successful one is, but who one is that counts. As in the example of Jesus, one's lifework can be completely destroyed and still one's life can be an immense success. Indeed, the destruction of one's lifework is one of the classic ways through which God brings his servants to their final surrender. The spiritual journey becomes more demanding as it unfolds, but also more liberating.

All creation is ours on the condition that we do not try to possess it. The innate desire to feel secure is an obstacle to enjoying all that exists. This does not mean that we are not to have possessions at all, but that we need to be detached from whatever we have. Otherwise, we lose the true perspective and, with it, the joy of this beatitude. John of the Cross wrote, "If you want to possess everything, desire to possess nothing."5 By cultivating a non-possessive attitude toward everything, including ourselves, everything is experienced as gift. Then one is truly poor in spirit and will find joy in everything.

A NEW KIND OF CONSCIOUSNESS

Jesus then came down with his apostles and stopped on some level ground. A large group of his disciples, besides a great many people from all over the Jewish country, including Jerusalem and from the seacoast of Tyre and Sidon, had come to hear him and be cured of their diseases. Everybody in the crowd endeavored to come and touch him and power was going out from him and healing everyone. It was then that he raised his eyes and fixed them upon his disciples and spoke as follows: "How blest are the poor in spirit; the reign of God is theirs. Blest are the meek; they shall inherit the land. Blest are the sorrowing; they shall be consoled." [Luke 6:17-20; Matt. 5:3-5]

In this rendering of the Sermon on the Mount, we are told that a great crowd had gathered. Many of the people had come to be healed of their diseases and had no concern for spiritual instruction. Jesus simply presented his teaching to everyone who happened to be present. We can be sure, therefore, that his words were also intended for us.

We saw that the poor in spirit are those afflicted for God's sake. People who are cut off from the normal symbols of security in society have the ideal disposition for the reign of God because they have nothing to lose. One who has nothing to lose obviously is much more willing to allow God into one's life. Jesus in his teaching suggests that the healing of our security center comes when we trust God to take care of all our needs. In the Sermon on the Mount, Jesus elaborates on what he means by letting go of the anxious search for more and more possessions to assuage our feelings of insecurity:

> Do not fret about what to eat and what to drink or about what to wear on your bodies. Is not life more precious than clothing? Look at the birds. They don't sow or reap or store provisions in barns, yet your heavenly Father feeds them. Observe the lilies of the field, how they grow. They do not toil or spin, yet even Solomon in all his glory did not dress like one of these.[6]

"Blest are the sorrowing; they shall be consoled." Love distorted by selfishness wants to cling to ephemeral or illusory projects for happiness. When we let such things go, we are bound to feel loss and the corresponding emotion of sorrow. This sorrow is not the same as that which comes from the unwillingness to let go of what is being asked or taken from us and which may give rise to discouragement, depression and even despair. The willingness to let go and bear the loss of what we love gives rise to a new inner freedom that enables us to live without what we previously thought was so essential. That freedom with its accompanying peace is the consolation that is promised in this beatitude. We have to allow for the grieving period to run its course and not run away from it. Nor should we think there is something wrong if we sometimes cast a backward glance at something we left behind or are overtaken at times by a backlash of emotional turmoil. In actual fact, we never lose anything that truly deserves to be loved; we simply enter into a more mature relationship with it.

"Blest are the meek; they shall inherit the land." The meek are those who do not get angry in the face of insult or injury and who have begun to dismantle their need or demand to control other people, events, and their own lives. When they experience an insult or humiliation, they do not feel it as a loss of power. Hence, they are free to continue to show love. The meek refuse to injure others regardless of the provocation. They are not judgmental. They may not approve of someone's conduct or principles, but they refuse to make a moral judgment about the person in question. Rather, their freedom from their power/control center enables them to have great compassion for those who are still imprisoned in the straightjacket of power needs that never rest and that can never be fulfilled.

The teaching of Gandhi, who preached *ahimsa* (usually translated as "the practice of nonviolence"), points to a new kind of consciousness in which, instead of returning an eye for an eye and a tooth for a tooth, one goes on showing love. *Ahimsa* is not a passive attitude but one that actively shows love no matter what happens. The love is so delicate and sincere that it refuses to take advantage of one's persecutor when he is vulnerable.

The meekness proposed in this beatitude is not passivity but the firm determination to go on loving no matter what evil another person does to us. It believes that to show love is the true nature of being human. This behavior undercuts violence at its roots. Violence tends to beget violence. When people feel attacked, they defend themselves. There is no end to the chain of violence until one of the contenders refuses to respond in kind. The determination to go on loving in spite of immense provocation is the only way to achieve peace among families, communities and nations. It presupposes and manifests the inner freedom to which the Gospel invites us.

OUT REACH

Jesus now entered Jericho. As he made his way through the town, there was a stir. A man named Zacchaeus, a high official among the tax collectors and rich as well, was curious to find out who Jesus was, but owing to the press of people, had no chance to do so, for he was small of stature. In order, therefore, to get a glimpse of Jesus, he ran ahead and climbed a sycamore tree because Jesus was expected to pass that way.

When Jesus came to the spot, he looked up. "Zacchaeus," he said to him, "come down quickly. Today I must be your guest." Coming down quickly, he welcomed him joyfully. A murmur ran through the crowd of spectators. "He has turned in," they commented, "to accept the hospitality of a sinner." Then Zacchaeus drew himself up and addressed the Lord, "Upon my word, Lord, I give to the poor one-half of my possessions, and if I have obtained anything from anybody by extortion, I will refund four times as much."

Then in his presence Jesus said, "Today salvation has visited this household because he, too, is the son of Abraham. After all, it is the mission of the son of man to seek and to save what is lost." [Luke 19:1-10][7]

This Gospel about Zacchaeus is a practical example of two of the beatitudes. "How happy are they who hunger and thirst after holiness for they shall be fully satisfied" refers to life without the tyranny of the false-self system. It heralds graduation from the emotional programs of early childhood, whose force or cutting edge has been blunted by the discipline of contemplative prayer. The fruits of that discipline manifest themselves in the determination to practice what is characteristic of this level of human consciousness, which is to show love. Divine love is not mere feeling; it is the love that manifests itself by deeds.

The primary sacrament of Christianity is Jesus himself. A sacrament is a visible sign of the invisible presence of grace; it communicates and transmits what it signifies. Jesus transmitted what he signified, divine love, by his teaching and example. He manifested how the divine nature functions. He revealed that the inner life of God is sheer gift: surrender that tends to throw itself away. The humility of God is to cease to be God. Within the Trinity there is the total emptying of the Father into the Son and the Son into the Father. What binds them together is the Spirit, the mutual love of the Father and the Son. Each member of the Trinity lives in the others rather than in itself. This is what is meant by "Tri-Unity": one divine nature possessed by three different Relationships. Relationship is the only distinction in God, but it is infinite. Thus, in the Trinity there is infinite Unity and infinite diversity because of the unique relationship of each member to the divine nature. Jesus manifests this unity insofar as it can be manifested in a human being.

After Jesus, the greatest sacrament is another human being. We are made in the image and likeness of God. Moreover, those who have been taken up through faith and baptism into the Body of Christ are growing as a corporate personality into the fullness of Christ. Paul calls this the

Mystery that has been hidden from the beginning of the world and which is now revealed in Jesus Christ. To hunger and thirst after justice is to manifest divine love under all circumstances. This is what human beings were created to do. It is our nature. Everything else is unnatural; any other disposition is abnormal.

The next beatitude, "Blessed are they who show mercy; mercy shall be theirs," describes the result of moving beyond selfish- ness into the love that is totally self-giving. It is the imitation of Christ and the fulfillment of the new commandment "to love one another as I have loved you." This means to love people not only in their hidden beauty as members of Christ, but in their concreteness and individuality; that is, in their personality traits, idiosyncracies and opinions which we may find irritating or unbearable. Even in the face of persecution and injury, if one enjoys the inner freedom of this beatitude, one continues to show love.

How do we show love in the concrete? How do we build up society when we have our own problems that scarcely leave us enough time or resources to take care of our own family, business, or spiritual life? As the consciousness of the inequalities in the world increases, the question of personal responsibility emerges with ever-increasing urgency. The nations of the West use up most of the world's resources while the rest of the world has barely enough to subsist on. As individuals, we may feel overwhelmed by the injustice in the world. We are painfully aware that the greed of human beings is the cause of starvation. We realize that if the global community was ordered properly and technology were shared equally, no one would go hungry even for a day. We ask what it means to show love when we do not know how to team up with others to alter governments, institutions and economies that take no interest in the equitable distribution of the earth's goods. Our frustration level rises as we feel unable to effect any change.

The author of *Caring for Society*[8] tells the story of a young couple managing a catering service. While taking part in a prison ministry, they heard about an inmate who was about to be released and needed a job. They talked it over and decided to offer him a job in their business. They were uneasy about how he would work out, but felt inspired to offer him this opportunity, so they hired him to deliver food to their clients. When it became known that he was an ex-convict, a number of the customers became uneasy also and decided to make use of another catering service. The couple began to lose money and eventually had to close down. Instead of firing their employee, they started another catering business and integrated him into it. Their new business became a bigger success than the former one. Showing mercy is actually the best investment one can make. Failures and losses may be God's way of getting us into a better situation.

Zacchaeus was a representative of the despised profession of tax collectors, generally considered to be the worst of sinners. When Jesus came to Jericho, this little man climbed a sycamore tree to get a better view of him. Jesus looked up at Zacchaeus and said, "I want to stay at your house." Zacchaeus was delighted. He shimmied down the tree and welcomed Jesus into his home. Preparing a great feast, he invited all his disreputable friends and staged a party.

After a few cups of wine, the little man, pleased to have Jesus in his house, pulled himself up to his full height and announced, "I give half of my possessions to the poor. If I have extorted money from anyone, I pay back four times over." Thus he freely admitted the unethical character of some of his financial success. Jesus' reply was, "Today, salvation has visited this household." Because Zacchaeus had welcomed Jesus into his house and not just watched him pass by, he had been changed. Salvation had entered his house through the gift of hospitality.

This is exactly what the couple did in our story. They could have watched while other people tried to find a position for the ex-convict. They heard Jesus' request as he was passing by, "Will you invite me into your house?" And they invited him in.

The inner movement to reach out to someone in need is the inspiration of the Spirit. To respond, one has to take the first step and show love in some small but practical, concrete way. If you hunger and thirst for holiness, the opportunities for practicing this beatitude will multiply.

Jesus' encounter with Zacchaeus is a wisdom teaching meaning, "If you want to practice love, observe the opportunities that are right in front of your noses."

THE HIGHER DEGREES OF HAPPINESS

Blest are the single-hearted; for they shall see God. Blest are the peacemakers; they shall be called children of God. [Matt. 5:6-9]

The opportunities for satisfying the hunger for holiness are immediately at hand if we are sensitive to the needs of others. Every now and then we are prompted to offer some kind of assistance at considerable cost to ourselves. This offer has to be appropriate to our state of life; at the same time, it challenges us to go beyond our routines and preconceptions, and to reach out to someone needing special care. This is the inspiration that leads to the beatitude of the merciful, which is to put into practice our contemplative vision.

The dialogue between our contemplative vision and how we incarnate it is the subject of the next beatitude, "Blest are the single-hearted for they shall see God." The single-hearted see God in themselves, in others and in the ordinary events of life. Jesus said, "The Son cannot do anything by himself — he can only do what he sees the Father doing."[9] Thus, he is always looking at the Father. What Jesus does is to translate his vision of the Father into his daily life and teaching and ultimately into his passion and death on the cross. This is an important point for our practice. Contemplative prayer is the place of encounter between the creative vision of transformation and the actual incarnation of that vision day by day. Practice is the translation of the creative vision into the concrete circumstances of each day.

It must be emphasized over and over that daily life is the fundamental practice. Hence, the incarnation of our vision — how we live it — is of supreme importance. If we are not available for daily encounter with God in contemplative prayer, the dynamic dialogue between the creative vision and its practical incarnation will be missing in our lives; or at least it will not pass through the intimate discerning experience of contemplative prayer. To bring both our activity and our vision together in vital dialogue is to perceive the right way of manifesting that vision *today.* Maybe it will be a little different tomorrow. We must not respond to Christ in a static way — with one set of resolutions or with the same set of tools all the time. Our practice has to be adjusted as we keep climbing the spiral ascent that the beatitudes describe. The eagle circles as it rises toward the sun. The same movement is present in the beatitudes. As we circle around the creative vision and see different aspects of it, our understanding is enhanced. In addition to circling on the horizontal plane as we negotiate the spiral ascent, we also perceive reality on the vertical plane from ever higher perspectives.

To emphasize only the contemplative vision is to risk stagnating in one's spiritual evolution. To emphasize only its incarnation is to risk becoming drained, or even to lose the vision itself. Hence, the necessity of bringing the two together every day in confrontation and dialogue. Every day is a new unfolding of our life in Christ. Surprises are always happening. God reserves the right to intrude into our lives at a moment's notice, sometimes turning them upside-down. It is essential to be flexible, adjustable, ready to tear up our plans and put them in the wastebasket at God's request. Hence, both the contemplative vision and its incarnation are essential, and the place where they meet is contemplative prayer. This is the key to the preservation and growth of the creative vision as well as its appropriate incarnation on a day-to-day basis. This is what leads to purity of heart, which is freedom from the false-self system and hence, freedom to be at the disposal of God and those we serve.

The beatitude of the peacemakers reveals that the peacemaker is one who has established peace within oneself. Peace is not a naive simplicity, but the perfect harmony of immense complexity. It is the delicate balance between all the faculties of human nature totally subject to God's will and transformed by divine love into a finely tuned instrument.

Peacemaking is the normal overflow of rootedness in Christ. Peacemakers are those who have the assurance of being the children of God. They are the ones who in a sense are God acting in the world. They pour into the world the being they have received from God, which is a share in his divine nature.

Today, God seems to be urging us to take more initiative in dealing with global problems and to take part in the transformation of society, beginning, of course, with what is closest to us. A creative vision releases an enormous amount of energy and can transform society beyond our wildest dreams. Divine empowerment is more present in those who climb the ladder of the beatitudes than anywhere else in creation. The power of the stars is nothing compared to the energy of a person whose will has been freed from the false-self system and who is thus enabled to co-create the cosmos together with God. God's top priority is the creation of a world in which the goods of the earth are equitably distributed, where no one is forgotten or left out, and where no one can rest until everyone has enough to eat, the oppressed have been liberated, and justice and peace are the norm among the nations and religions of the world. Until then, even the joy of transforming union is incomplete. The commitment to the spiritual journey is not a commitment to pure joy, but to taking responsibility for the whole human family, its needs and destiny. We are not our own; we belong to everyone else.

THE ULTIMATE BEATITUDE

Jesus said to his disciples: To you who hear me, I say: Love your enemies, do good to those who hate you; bless those who curse you and pray for those who maltreat you. When someone slaps you on one cheek, turn and give him the other; when someone takes your coat, let him have your shirt as well. Give to all who beg from you. When a man takes what is yours, do not demand it back. Do to others what you would have them do to you.

If you love those who love you, what credit is that to you? Even sinners love those who love them. If you do good to those who do good to you, how can you claim any credit? Sinners do as much. If you lend to those from whom you expect repayment, what merit is there in it for you? Even sinners lend to sinners, expecting to be repaid in full.

Love your enemy and do good; lend without expecting repayment. Then will your recompense be great. You will rightly be called sons of the Most High, since He Himself is good to the ungrateful and the wicked.

Be compassionate, as your Father is compassionate. Do not judge, and you will not be judged. Do not condemn, and you will not be condemned. Pardon, and you shall be pardoned. Give, and it shall be given to you. Good measure pressed down, shaken together, running over, will they pour into the fold of your garment. For the measure you measure with will be measured back to you. [Luke 6:27-38][10]

Humility is a relationship of honesty to everything: to God, oneself, other people and all reality. God is selfless love, giving to the point of emptying himself and trying not to be God. It is a great gift to be detached from this world's goods; it is a still greater gift to be detached from all spiritual goods. This is the way that God relates to us: not interested in his own majesty or transcendence, but trying to be nobody — without, of course, much success. It must be fun when you are everything to be nothing. In any case, his disposition to give away everything that he has or is, seems to characterize the divine goodness and compassion.

This is the disposition that Jesus invites us to imitate on the mountainside in his seemingly casual sermon. Jesus urges us to have the freedom not to harbor a possessive attitude toward anything, including oneself; to be, without wanting to be anything special; and to be one with everything that is, in an all-inclusive attitude of belonging and sharing. One of the examples of this attitude is lending without hope of return. Actually, from the perspective of the beatitudes, one is only lending to oneself. Again, there is no sense in judging others because that would be judging oneself. This disposition of giving everything away — one's time, energy, space, virtues, spirituality, and finally oneself — is not really giving anything away because, in the truest sense, whatever we give away, we are giving to ourselves. The gesture of opening one's hand is the same gesture as receiving.

This emptying of ourselves for the good of others is a continuation of the same movement of emptying — *kenosis* — that goes on in the Trinity: giving away (or throwing away) all that the Father is to the Son and vice-versa, and each receiving everything back in and through the Person of infinite love, the Holy Spirit. As one manifests this love, one is giving everything away and receiving everything in return again and again, but each time with greater inclusiveness. The same love that one gives away keeps coming back, "Good measure pressed down, shaken together, running over."[11] In the same degree that love goes forth, it returns into our lap. This compassionate, non-judgmental, selfless love is the Source of all that is; the ultimate beatitude is to disappear into it.

THE PARABLES

It is one thing to communicate to others conclusions and admonitions based on one's profound spiritual experience . . . It is quite another thing to try to communicate that experience itself, or better, to assist people to find their own ultimate encounter. This is what the parables of Jesus seek to do: to help others into their own experience of the Reign of God and to draw from that experience *their own way of life*.[12]

THE REIGN OF GOD

Jesus proposed to the crowd another parable: The reign of God may be likened to the man who sowed good seed in his field. While everyone else was asleep, his enemy came and sowed weeds among the wheat and then made off. When the crop began

to mature and yield grain the weeds made their appearance as
well. The owner's slaves came to him and said, "Sir, did you
not sow good seed in your field? Where are the weeds coming
from?" He answered, "I see an enemy's hand in this." The slave
said to him, "Do you want us to go out and pull them up?" "No,"
he replied, "Pull up the weeds and you might take the wheat
along with them. Let them grow together until harvest. Then
at harvest time I will order the harvesters: 'First collect the weeds
and bundle them to burn. Then gather the wheat into my barn.'"

He proposed still another parable: The reign of God is like
a mustard seed which someone took and sowed in his field. It
is the smallest seed of all, yet when full-grown it is the largest
of plants. It becomes so big that the birds of the sky come and
build their nests in its branches.

He offered them still another image: The reign of God is
like yeast which a woman took and kneaded into three measures
of flour. Eventually the whole mass of dough began to rise.

All these lessons Jesus taught to the crowd in the form of
parables. He spoke to them in parables only to fulfill what had
been said through the prophet: "I will open my mouth in parables;
I will announce what has lain hidden since the creation of the
world." [Matt. 13:24-35][13]

The parables reveal Jesus as a wisdom teacher of extraordinary qualities.
In order to understand his teaching, we need to understand the nature of
what he calls the reign (or kingdom) of God. The reign (or kingdom) of
God does not consist of a place, a form of government, or even of the rule
of God over our actions and interior life. It is not an organization into which
we are supposed to fit. It generally introduces itself by an event (or a series
of events) that changes our lives. Many of the parables describe situations
in which someone's life is suddenly turned upside-down. In these parables
Jesus seems to say that this intrusion into one's life is how the reign of God
manifests itself. To allow one's life to be turned upside-down requires a
change of heart. And a change of heart presupposes a certain disenchantment
with what we have been considering happiness.

The parables were directed to people who were just coming out of their
selfish programs for happiness and becoming aware that there is an alternative.
It is not easy to let go of what we believe to be essential to our happiness
even for the sake of participating in God's reign or kingdom.

At the beginning of our conversion most of us experience the gnawing sensation of wanting to move more deeply into the reign of God and to be able to find it in daily life. At the same time, we want to hang onto our emotional routines, fixations, ways of looking at things and our commentaries on people and events that exasperate us. These three parables offer encouragement to those who are beginning the path or struggling along it.

The reign of God is not so much what we do under God's inspiration as what the divine action does in us, with or without our cooperation. The reign of God often is disruptive, to judge by many of the parables. One day Jesus told a parable about a day laborer who was digging in a field and found hidden treasure.[14] With the endless movement of armies throughout the Holy Land during the pre-Gospel period, people often hid their valuables in open fields with the hope of coming back later and recovering them. So it was not extraordinary for someone digging in a field to come upon a hidden treasure. The parable concludes: "Immediately, he went and sold everything he had and bought that field." I suppose he built a mansion somewhere. His good luck changed his life. He was no longer a day laborer.

In another parable, Jesus recounted the story of a man who was in the jewelry business. One day he found a pearl of great price, so he sold everything he had and bought that pearl.[15] This purchase changed his life in much the same way that winning in the state lottery today completely changes a person's life-style. The reign of God breaks into the course of our ordinary occupations, business or family life and changes things around. It is what we do with that intrusion that determines whether we enter or belong to the reign of God or not. The willingness to allow God to walk into our lives, tear up our plans and throw them in the wastebasket is a good beginning.

These two parables emphasize the fact that the reign of God is what happens. It is not any one thing that happens. It is the fact of God's entering our lives at any moment and shifting things around, and our consenting to the break-in. Once we have found "the pearl of great price" or "the treasure hidden in a field", a conflict arises between our desire to be open to the continuing intrusions of the reign of God and our habitual unwillingness to change or be changed. What do we do with that? The three parables in the present text offer insight and encouragement.

A householder of apparent wealth sowed wheat in his field. Shortly there appeared a "weed". This weed was not just any kind of weed; it was darnel, which is the spitting image of wheat. It is very hard to distinguish the two. The zealous farmhands asked the householder how this mischance had come to be. He said, "An enemy has done this." They asked, "Shall we pull out the weeds?"

"No," he replied, "let them grow until the proper time. Then we will have the harvest and separate the two, lest in pulling up the weeds, we lose some of the wheat."

This parable is a warning to over-zealous reformers to go at a pace that will not destroy the good even if it is mixed up with a lot of evil. There will always be a mixture of good and evil in everything until the end of the world. The parable reminds us that we must put up with the evil in ourselves and have a friendly attitude toward our weaknesses. We feel the attraction of grace to move to an ever-deepening spiritual commitment to God, but our resolutions seem so tenuous at times that we fear we may lose them.

But Jesus seems to be saying, "Don't worry about it." God expects that we will experience confusion and weakness. We may at times be unable to discern where our attitudes and actions are coming from, but the parable implies that the wheat is more powerful than the weeds and will eventually win. At some point in our spiritual journey we will be ready for the separation of the wheat from the chaff. God warns us to give the crop time to mature and to leave the harvest to him.

The parable about the mustard seed suggests a positive view of the conflict. The mustard seed is one of the tiniest and most insignificant of all seeds, but when it is put into the ground and allowed to grow to maturity, it turns into the biggest of all shrubs. Birds come and build their nests in it. The message is that the reign of God, like the germinating mustard seed, is incredibly powerful even though its energy is out of reach of our faculties. Though it seems insignificant to us and we feel overwhelmed by the density of the weeds, we should have no fear. With time the seed time will grow in spite of the difficulties that seem to be overwhelming it.

The third parable is about the yeast in the dough. Yeast is a living organism and requires water to be activated. The activating principle in the reign of God is faith. The consent of faith to the divine action is at first hidden from our psyche. So, too, yeast is hard to identify when it is hidden in the dough, but its inherent power gradually causes the dough to rise. Similarly, the reign of God has the power to transform; it changes us into something new.

Jesus lays out the principles, offers the invitation, gives encouragement and finally appeals to our freedom: "If you wish, the reign of God is yours. But you have to take the responsibility of deciding. If you choose to enter it, you have nothing to worry about. The evil in you will not overcome the good that has been sown. At some point, the life you now experience with so much conflict will be transformed, and all the evils that weigh you down will disappear."

THE TALENTS

Jesus presented this parable to the crowd. Imagine a man who, before going abroad, sent for his officials and entrusted his money to them. Then he gave five talents to one, to another he gave two, and to a third, just one; to each the amount proportioned to his individual ability. He then went abroad. At once, the recipient of the five talents went to invest them in enterprise and made another five. In like manner, the recipient of the two talents made another two. But the recipient of the one talent went away to dig a hole in the ground and buried his master's money. After a long delay, the master of those officials returned and settled accounts with them. So the recipient of the five talents came forward and presented five additional talents. "Master," he said, "you entrusted me with five talents. Look, I made another five." "Well done, good and faithful servant," the master said to him. "You were faithful in managing something small. I will now put you in charge of something great. Share to the full your master's happiness."

When the recipient of the two talents came, he said in turn, "Master, you entrusted me with two talents. Look, I made another two." "Well done, good and faithful servant," the master said to him. "You were faithful in managing something small. I will now put you in charge of something great. Share to the full your master's happiness."

Finally the recipient of the one talent came before him and said, "Master, I know you are a hard taskmaster. You reap where you have not sown and you store away what you have not winnowed. So I shrank from doing anything at all and went to bury your talent in the ground. Here, you have your capital back again."

But his master had an answer for him. "You lazy good-for-nothing fellow," he said to him, "you knew that I reap where I have not sown and store away what I have winnowed. Then you ought to have put my money in the bank and on my return I might have at least recovered my capital plus the interest. Therefore, take the talent away from him and give it to the one who has the ten talents. Everyone who already has will receive more yet till he abounds in wealth, while the one who does not have will lose even what he has." [Matt. 25:14-29]¹⁶

According to contemporary exegetes, the parables are the most authentic part of the Gospel. Their repetitive quality helps the memory retain and repeat them with ease. Almost all the parables are designed to shake up the values of the people who are listening and to invite them to reflect on what their values actually are.

In the parable of the Good Samaritan, a priest and levite pass by a man who had been beaten up by robbers and left by the roadside. Both go to the other side of the road to avoid getting close to him. The Good Samaritan takes care of the victim, puts him in a hostel, pays for his food, binds up his wounds, and even leaves some money behind so that he can be properly cared for until the Samaritan can come back. In the minds of the people hearing this story, the Samaritans were the scum of the earth. The paradox of a Samaritan doing the right thing and two respectable religious figures doing the wrong thing forces the listeners to reflect. The reversal of their expectations invites them to raise questions about their own motivation and values.

We might think that the man who hid his talent in the ground was a smart fellow. After all, wouldn't we do the same thing if we felt we were not astute in business? Suppose the man had invested his only talent and lost it through a poor investment. He would have had nothing. He hid it in the ground so that he could at least return it to his master. As he later explained, "I was afraid that I wouldn't do a good job of investing your money. Knowing that you are a hard taskmaster, I hid it in the ground to be sure that I would have it to give back to you upon your return. Here it is."

The master, instead of being grateful, grabbed the money out of his hand, shouting, "You lousy good-for-nothing! Get out of my sight!" Then he gave the money to the one who already possessed ten talents. We are left wondering what the man did to deserve such wrath. Is it better to take a risk or to protect what we have received?

The Gospel invites us to holiness and higher states of consciousness. This invitation involves risk; it means growing beyond where we are. It asks us to invest our talents even when we feel they are inadequate to a particular situation, job or ministry. It means that God, when he calls us to ministry, does not promise success, especially immediate success.

The parable of the talents shows what happens to two people who accepted God's invitation. They worked hard and with God's help, doubled their investment. The man who hid his talent in the ground is like those who opt for the status quo because they know what it is; they are unwilling to open themselves to the risks of the spiritual journey. They refuse to work at the potential that God has given them and thus obstruct the upward evolution of the human family. Even if they do not regress to lower levels of consciousness, they fail to support the development of human consciousness into Christ-consciousness.

The man in the parable chose security as his happiness project and in so doing, closed himself off from the opportunity of further growth. Hence, the judgment: "Take away his talent and give it to those who are already advancing."

Notice that the parable of the talents is taken from the business world. All the parables are based upon ordinary events: some from business, for the sake of the urban population; some from farming or fishing, for the sake of the rural population. Cooking, sweeping, lighting lamps, sewing, harvesting, investing, going to the bank — these daily occurrences form the basis of the parables. This suggests that everyday life is the place where the reign of God takes place. We don't have to go to a monastery, convent, or hermitage. We do not have to go anywhere because the reign of God is right in front of our eyes. It is "close at hand." Divine union is available to everyone on the face of the earth. Our potential for divine union is the talent, above every other, that must not be hidden in the ground.

The experience of trying and failing is the way to learn to discard self-centered programs for happiness and to surrender to the movement of transformation. Sin is the refusal to continue to evolve. By clinging to mere survival and security, we withdraw ourselves and others from the opportunity and adventure of continuing to grow into the body of Christ.

INCIDENTS FROM JESUS' MINISTRY

In the afterglow of Pentecost, we celebrate the historical life of Jesus in the light of our experience of the Spirit, who introduces us to the trans-historical life of Jesus. In this perspective, grace is the presence and action of Christ in our lives right now, and the Gospel texts are mirrors reflecting back to us the same presence and action of Christ in the lives of his disciples.

PETER AT CAPERNAUM

The disciples and Jesus now entered Capernaum whereon, the very next Sabbath, he went to the synagogue to teach. Immediately after that they went to the house of Simon and Andrew. Now Simon's mother-in-law lay in bed with a fever and they at once appealed to him on her behalf. He approached and taking her by the hand, raised her up and set her on her feet. The fever left her and she waited on them.

Late in the evening after the sun had set, all the sick as well as possessed persons were brought to him. Presently the whole town was assembled at the door. He cured many that were suffering from various diseases.

Very early the next morning, while it was still dark, he rose, left the house and went to an out-of-the-way place, and there he prayed. Simon and his companions went in pursuit of him and when they found him said to him, "Everyone is looking for you."

He replied, "Let us go elsewhere and visit the neighboring hamlets. I want to preach there too. That is the purpose of my mission." [Mark 1:21, 29-39][17]

The spiritual journey is God's idea. We did not invent it. Nor did we choose ourselves as candidates for it. God chose us. Of course, He doesn't call us on the phone and say, "I have made a reservation for you." Through the various circumstances in our lives, doors open and close. It is not we who are pursuing God, but God who is pursuing us. Every effort we make to go to God is a lowering of our defenses against the divine approach. God surrounds us with infinite mercy like sunshine. But we tend to keep the curtains at our windows closed, occasionally opening them ajar to let in just a tiny ray of light. If we chose to, we could yank open the heavy drapes, and find ourselves bathed in light!

Peter is presented in the Gospel as one of the more unreliable and unstable of Jesus' followers. Nobody but Jesus would have thought of making him an apostle. Peter wanted all the things that worldly people want, only transposed into a religious context.

One day Jesus entered Peter's hometown and walked down the main street. A man like Peter was impressed when Jesus stopped at his house and said, "We'll stay here." But then Peter discovered that his mother-in-law was sick with a fever. "My God," he thought, "of all the days for that woman to get sick, why does she have to choose this one?"

Jesus noticed Peter's discomfort, went upstairs, took the woman by the hand and set her on her feet. Whereupon she came down and prepared a meal that was a smashing success. Everyone was aglow with the festivities when the whole town started coming to Peter's doorstep, bringing the sick to be healed. Jesus went out and healed them all.

Everybody went to bed in high spirits. Jesus got up early in the morning and slipped away to pray in solitude. It did not take Peter long to realize that he had disappeared. The local equivalent of the rotary club noticed his disappearance too. They hastened to Peter and said, "What are we going to do? We can't lose this important man! Think what it would mean for our town if he makes this his headquarters. He worked miracles at your doorstep; he healed your mother-in-law. You're the man to go and bring him back!"

Accordingly, a delegation with Peter at its head was sent in pursuit of Jesus. When they found him, Peter blurted out, "Everybody is looking for you!" He might have added, "If you come back, we'll build you a synagogue and a house! We'll set up concessions and you'll get a share of the revenues."

Jesus replied, "Let us go someplace else." Notice the word "us," that is, "you and me." It is as if Jesus was saying, "I don't care what other people think of me. What I'm interested in is, what do *you* think of me? Are you willing to go where I want to go rather than where you want me to go?"

LAUNCHING OUT INTO DEEP WATERS

One day the crowd was surging up against Jesus and listening to the word of God. While he was standing on the beach of Lake Gennesaret, he saw two boats drawn up on the beach. The fishermen had disembarked and were washing their nets. After entering one of the boats, which belonged to Simon, he asked them to push out a little from the shore. He then sat down and taught the crowds from the boat.

When he had finished speaking, he said to Simon, "Launch out into the deep water and have your men lower the net for a haul."

"Master," Simon said, "we worked all night without catching a thing. However, since you tell us to do so, I will have the nets let down." When they had done this, they caught in a single haul an extraordinary number of fish. In fact their nets threatened to break. They beckoned to their partners in the other boat to come and lend them a hand. They came and both boats were filled so that they were on the point of sinking.

When Simon Peter saw what had happened, he threw himself down at the feet of Jesus and said, "Lord, leave my boat, for I am a sinful man." A feeling of awe had gripped him, as it had all his associates, because of the number of fish caught in the haul. So, too, it had seized James and John, the sons of Zebedee who were Simon's partners.

Jesus then said to Simon, "You have nothing to fear. Hereafter you will be a fisher of people."

When they had brought the boat to shore, they abandoned everything and became his followers. [Luke 5:1-11][18]

Peter was not ready to leave his hometown and returned to his fishing business. Jesus, however, continued to show interest in him. One day, Jesus was at the shore of the lake teaching a large crowd. He looked around and saw several boats along the shore. He could have gotten into one of several boats, but he chose to get into Peter's and to preach from there.

After preaching at length to the people, Jesus turned to Peter and said, "Launch out into the deep waters and ask your men to put down their nets for a catch." This was not a welcome suggestion. The little fishing company had been up all night and had caught nothing.

The fishermen took to their oars, rowed out into the middle of the lake and lowered their nets. Suddenly a school of fish swam into their nets. The boat started listing to one side, and they had to call to their companions in another boat for help. Both boats were filled with so many fish that they were at the point of sinking. When they finally got to shore and what had happened fully dawned on Peter, his eyes grew bigger and bigger. He threw himself at the feet of Jesus saying, "Leave my boat, for I am a sinful man." A feeling of awe had gripped him. Jesus said to him, "Don't be afraid. I will make you a fisher of people."

Notice that it was while plying his trade that Peter was finally converted. God generally approaches us where we are: with children who are unmanageable, with a spouse who is late for supper, or with relatives who are unbearable.

PETER AT LAKE GENNESARET

After the miraculous multiplication of the loaves and fishes, Jesus obliged the disciples to re-enter a boat and precede him to the other shore while he would dismiss the crowds. After dismissing them, he went up the mountainside alone to pray. Night fell and he was still there alone while the boat was far out at sea. It was hit hard by the waves since the wind was against them. During the last part of the night, however, he came toward them, walking over the sea. When they saw him walk upon the sea, they were perplexed. "It is a ghost!" they said, and from fright cried out. Jesus at once addressed them. "Take heart," he said, "it is I. Do not be afraid."

Thus reassured, Peter said to him, "Master, if it is you, tell me to come to you over the water."

"Come," he replied. So Peter climbed out and started in the direction of Jesus, walking over the water. But when he felt the stiff breeze, he took alarm, and when he began to sink, cried out, "Lord, save me!" Jesus immediately reached out his hand and took hold of him. "How little faith you have," he said to him. "What made you doubt?"

Then they climbed up into the boat and the wind subsided. The men in the boat prostrated themselves before him and said, "You are indeed the Son of God." [Matt. 14:22-33][19]

Having dismissed the crowd, Jesus went off to pray in solitude. While absorbed in God, he did not notice that a storm had arisen on the lake and that his disciples, whom he had sent off to the other shore, were being bounced around by the waves and the wind. The disciples were rowing with all their might but were not making any headway. Jesus started coming to them walking on the water. They thought he was a ghost! Jesus reassured them, "Don't be afraid. It is I."

The words, "Don't be afraid," seem to have served as a bugle call in Peter's ears, and he responded, "Master, if it is you, tell me to come to you over the water!"

Jesus could have said, "Stay in the boat. We don't want to have two ghosts walking on the water." Instead, Jesus called back, "Come!"

When Peter, after a few steps, began to sink, Jesus reached out and pulled him out of the water. As soon as they were back in the boat, Jesus said, "How little faith you have! What made you doubt?" There is nothing like humiliation and failure, especially when witnessed by our peers, to help us face up to our motivation and to ask important questions: Why did you do it? Excessive desires for security and survival, affection and esteem, and power and control are out-of-date motives as far as the Gospel is concerned. Since Peter was deeply enmeshed in them, this was a crucial experience for him. It challenged him to change the direction in which he was looking for happiness and in particular, to stop seeking the esteem of others.

THE MISSION OF THE SEVENTY-TWO

After these incidents, the Lord appointed another group, seventy-two in all, and sent them out two-by-two to go ahead of him to every town and place where he intended to visit personally. He said to them, "The harvest is plentiful but the laborers are few. Pray the owner of the harvest, therefore, to send out laborers to do his harvesting. Go now, but mind you, I am sending you out like lambs among a pack of wolves. Do not burden yourselves with purse or bag or sandals and greet no one by the way. Whatever house you enter, the first thing you say must be a blessing on this house. Make your headquarters in just that house and eat and drink whatever they have to offer. Do not be constantly shifting from house to house. Whatever

town you enter, if the people make you welcome, eat what is
set before you, take care of the sick in the place and speak to
the inhabitants on this theme: 'The Kingdom of God has finally
come to you.'"

The seventy-two returned in high spirits. "Master," they said,
"even the demons are subject to us because we use your name."

"Yes," he said to them, "I was watching Satan fall like
lightning flashes from heaven. But, mind you, it is I that have
given you the power to tread upon serpents and scorpions and
break the dominion of the enemy everywhere. Just the same,
do not rejoice in the fact that the spirits are subject to you, but
rejoice in the fact that your names are engraved in Heaven."
[Luke 10:1-9; 17-20][20]

The miraculous haul of fish prompted Peter and his companions to
leave everything and to follow Jesus. Jesus then began to train the disciples
for their future ministries. In our text Jesus called together a group of seventy-
two and sent them out two-by-two, instructing them to preach the reign
of God and giving them the power to cure the sick and to cast out demons.
The actual exercise of these healing gifts must have been sensational. Perhaps
you are familiar with the healing services currently taking place in the
charismatic movement and are sometimes attended by thousands of people
and often lasting up to five or six hours. Scores of people are often healed.
Imagine the intense emotion and enthusiasm building up in such a service!

The disciples were evidently excited when, after a brief initiation into
the reign of God, they were able to heal diseases and cast out demons. They
came back in high spirits and poured out their success story to the Master:
"The demons are subject to us in your name!" Jesus gently put the lid on
their enthusiasm with these words: "It's good to work miracles, but don't
get too excited about such things. If you want to know what to get excited
about, it's that your names are written in heaven." With these words, he
shifted the focus of their enthusiasm from the natural satisfaction of success
to what apostolic ministry is actually based upon — the work of the Spirit
within us. Apostolic virtues come not from our natural talents but from
a mysterious emptying process in which our talents are put at the disposal
of the Spirit rather than of pride.

The disciples did not know what to do with Jesus' remarks; they had
to think them over. It is worth noting that Jesus sent these men out with
a special ministry so early in their formation, their fishing nets scarcely out

of their hands. In earlier times, it was generally believed that one should spend a long time in preparation for a special ministry, maybe even living an eremetical life for awhile. At the very least, it seemed necessary to go to a seminary or to join a monastery and subject oneself to an austere regime or to a highly disciplined lifestyle for a time. There is great merit in such a structured environment. Many famous missionaries enjoyed that kind of preparation for their ministries.

But here is the paradox. Whatever the value of such an approach to ministry, it is not the way that Jesus prepared his disciples. His method was similar to that of a swimming instructor who throws his students into the water. Jesus gave his disciples a ministry for which they were totally unprepared, knowing that they would enjoy a success for which they were even more unprepared.

In our day many ministries are emerging for lay folks that have not existed for centuries — counselors, administrators of parishes, liturgical ministers, justice and peace witnesses, social workers. These people often have to begin their ministries with little or no preparation. One wonders whether we should insist on adequate preparation or put more faith in the way that Jesus launched his disciples — jump in and see what happens. At least there was no danger of his disciples thinking that their success was due to their study of scripture, theology or the length of their preparation. The inexperienced disciples knew that their success could only have come from the empowerment that Jesus had given them.

In our day, there seems to be less and less time for a prolonged preparation for any ministry. The demands are great, the harvest is plentiful, and some ministries are so difficult that it would take a lifetime to prepare adequately for them.The only choice is to start ministering.

Thus the Gospel encourages the ministries of our time, but with this caution: *Don't expect success.* The seventy-two disciples had immediate success. Perhaps they were granted instant success because Jesus wanted them to realize their inability to handle it. In every ministry, success is normally accompanied sooner or later by trials, disappointments and failures.

In and through the ups and downs of ministry, God purifies the minister. Like the seventy-two disciples, he may throw us into a demanding form of service to let us find out right away that we can't do it on our own. A special mission is not a sign that we are holy; it is a challenge to become holy. The path to holiness is the experience of failure, and failure is certain if we are thrust into a form of ministry that we are not adequately prepared for. If we were fully prepared, it would be a lot easier on our families, friends, superiors and — above all — on our own self-image. As it is, people are bound to get upset with us — and we may become thoroughly discouraged with ourselves. We need to understand that we only grow in ministry through the experience of failure and humiliation. It is by becoming humble that one is able to practice ministry rightly, and humiliation is the path to humility.

In order to understand this teaching of Jesus more concretely, I offer the following tips. If you want to find out what a poor monk or nun you would make, join a monastery or convent. If you want to find out what a poor priest you would make, get yourself ordained. If you want to find out what a poor meditator you would make, start meditating. If you want to find out what a poor prayer you would make, try to pray. If you want to find out what a poor husband or wife you would make, find yourself a spouse.

When married couples experience marital difficulties, they think something is wrong with their spouse. When a priest experiences his inadequacies, he thinks the bishop is no good. When a monk or nun in a monastery enters the night of sense, they think something is wrong with the community: "If the rule was better observed, I would be perfect," they say; or, "If the superiors were reasonable, I would be in the seventh mansion with Teresa of Avila."

Love makes us vulnerable. The love of another person (including God) reduces our defense mechanisms. As soon as we trust somebody, we no longer have to be self-protective in their presence, and our defenses diminish. Then the faults and limitations that we have never seen or always tried to hide begin to emerge as clear as crystal for the benefit of our friends, relatives, colleagues and spouses. Such difficulties generally indicate that our particular ministry or relationship is working well.

Once we learn to accept failure, love grows. We do not grow by thinking about it or by wishing for it, but only through the experience of failure.

There are three stages of transformation that repeat themselves as we climb the spiritual ladder. The first step is human effort — the willingness to accept the invitation of Christ to undertake a ministry or relationship. The second is the inevitable result of doing something for which we are inadequate and unprepared — the experience of failure, which may be real or apparent, private or public. The final stage is the triumph of grace. One cannot predict it; one cannot demand it. All of a sudden, after one has persevered in the way of humiliation, the difficulties cease and one finds oneself in a new place. The experience of failure has taught us how to live and how to minister, which is to act with complete dependence on God.

There is no reason to get excited because we have a special ministry; it could be largely a question of natural endowment. We should rejoice, rather, because our names are written in heaven. We are part of God's unfolding plan to transform human consciousness. Our failures become the source of our strength according to Paul's formula, "When I am weak, then I am strong."[21] Christ will then empower us to minister to his people in ways that know no bounds.

On the other hand, if we make only a casual or an impermanent commitment to a ministry or to a marriage partner, we do not give enough time for the dynamic of self-knowledge to work. That dynamic gradually unveils the dark side of our personality and our false-self system with its self-centered programs for happiness that cannot possibly work.

In every vocation, events and other people constantly reactivate our emotional programs for happiness, along with the accompanying turmoil that occurs when these programs are frustrated. Such self-knowledge is not a disaster but the necessary condition for changing them. When these have been dismantled, our ministry starts to work of itself because, once freed from the obstacles of pride and subtle forms of selfishness that hold the false-self system in place, the Spirit of God can work in us.

The seventy-two disciples, flushed with success, came to the Lord expecting to get a pat on the back, and all he said was, "Don't get excited about working miracles. Anybody with a little psychic power can do that. What really counts is that you are part of God's plan. The thing to rejoice in is that you are chosen to become divine and to join me in raising the consciousness of the world."

Appendix 1

THE ROSARY

The joyful, sorrowful and glorious mysteries of the rosary are the mysteries of divine light, life and love that the liturgy celebrates from Advent to Epiphany, from Lent to the Ascension, and from Pentecost throughout the Sundays of Ordinary Time. Christmas is the feast of divine light and Epiphany is the fullness of it. Easter is the feast of divine life and Ascension is the fullness of it. Pentecost is the feast of divine love and the rest of the year is the expression of it. The revelation of divine light, life and love grows in proportion to the growth of faith, hope and charity, and vice-versa.

The rosary is a school of contemplative prayer. As the lips and hands are saying the beads and the mind is reflecting on the mysteries, the presence of Christ in our inmost being awakens and we rest in his presence. Whether we focus on the words of the individual prayers or reflect on the unfolding mysteries, we may feel drawn into this rest. At that time we leave behind both the words and the reflections and enjoy the presence of Christ. When his presence begins to dissolve, we return to the prayers and reflections where we left off. In this way, we move up and down the ladder of interior prayer and allow the habit of contemplation to develop. Contemplation gradually overflows into daily life and extends the enjoyment of God's presence into the whole of life.

Appendix 2

CONTEMPLATIVE LITURGY

For members of contemplative communities, the celebration of the Eucharist in a contemplative setting and mode is extremely refreshing. Shared silence is genuine liturgy. The practice of exterior and interior silence as an integral part of liturgy needs to be restored. Just as the Word of God emerges from the silence of the Father, so the sacred texts of the liturgy should emerge from the silence of the community. It is then that they achieve their full effect.

To prepare the congregation to worship in this fashion, a vestibule to pass from our external activity and preoccupations into the inner sanctuary of our hearts may be helpful and even necessary. The community of Taize has developed a series of chants which are available in English.[1] If one of these is chanted by the congregation for five or ten minutes at the beginning of the liturgy, preferably in four parts, a suitable atmosphere of recollection and prayer can be created.

After each lesson or group of lessons, a period of ten minutes of silence might be introduced. After the reception of the Eucharist, a similar period of silence, up to twenty minutes, might also be shared, depending on the amount of time at the disposal of the assembly. Hymns and sung responses are omitted and movements are reduced to a minimum. If the group is small, sitting around the altar table may help to sustain the atmosphere of recollection and silence.

The texts are read slowly and deliberately. The gestures of the celebrant and the words of the Eucharistic prayer are done with the utmost reverence and simplicity. A brief homily could invite the people to identify and commune with the presence of the risen Christ among them and within them.

Notes

PREFACE

1. 1 Cor. 2:16

2. 1 Col. 3:11

3. cf. Constitution on the Sacred Liturgy, *The Documents of Vatican II*, ed. by Walter Abbot, S.J., for description of the first four presences.

CHAPTER I

1. Gospel of Second Sunday of Advent

2. Gospel of Fourth Sunday of Advent

3. John 1:46

4. Gospel of Second Sunday in Ordinary Time

CHAPTER II

1. Gospel of the First Sunday of Lent

2. Romans 7:18-25 (*The Living New Testament*, Tyndale House Foundation, Wheaton, Ill.)

3. Gospel of the First Sunday of Lent

4. Gospel of the Second Sunday of Lent

5. Gospel of the Fourth Sunday of Lent

6. Gospel for Monday of Holy Week

7. From Jesus' final discourse at the Last Supper

8. John 10:30

9. Gal. 2:20

10. From the Gospel of Passion Sunday

11. Matt. 26:39

12. cf. Bernadette Roberts, *The Path to No-Self* and *The Experience of No-Self,* Shambhala, Boston, MA.

13. From the Gospel of Passion Sunday

14. Matt. 27:52-53

15. Gen. 1:3

16. From the Gospel of Good Friday

17. Ex. 3:7-8

18. Gospel for the Easter Vigil

19. Rev. 1:15

20. Tuesday of the Octave of Easter

21. Gospel of the Third Sunday of Easter

22. Gospel of the Third Sunday of Easter

23. Gospel of the Second Sunday of Easter

24. 2 Cor. 12:10

25. Gospel of the Third Sunday of Easter

26. Col. 3:11

CHAPTER III

1. John 20:22

2. Acts 1:4-5

3. John 3:8

4. John 17:22-23

5. John 7:37-38

6. John 17:21

CHAPTER IV

1. Gospel of Fourth Sunday in Ordinary Time

2. Gen. 1:27-31

3. John 1:46

4. Matt. 4:15

5. John of the Cross, *Ascent to Mt. Carmel*, Book I, Chapter 13, 11

6. Matt. 6:25-30

7. Gospel of 31st Sunday in Ordinary Time

8. Robert L. Kinast, *Caring for Society*, Thomas More Press, Chicago, IL, 1985

9. John 5:19

10. Gospel of Seventh Sunday in Ordinary Time

11. Luke 7:38

12. John Crossan, "In Parables," p. 52

13. Gospel of 16th Sunday in Ordinary Time

14. Matt. 13:44

15. Matt. 13:45

16. Gospel of 33rd Sunday in Ordinary Time

17. Gospel of Fifth Sunday in Ordinary Time

18. Gospel of Fifth Sunday in Ordinary Time

19. Gospel of 19th Sunday in Ordinary Time

20. Gospel of 14th Sunday in Ordinary Time

21. 1 Cor.

APPENDIX 2

1. *Music from Taize*, Vol. I and II, publ. by G.I.A. Publications, Inc., 7404 S. Mason Ave., Chicago, IL 60638